SIMULATION of SUICIDE BOMBING

SIMULATION of SUICIDE BOMBING

Using Computers to Save Lives

ZEESHAN-UL-HASSAN USMANI and **DANIEL KIRK**

iUniverse, Inc.

Bloomington

Simulation of Suicide Bombing
Using Computers to Save Lives

iUniverse books may be ordered through booksellers or by contacting:

iUniverse
1663 Liberty Drive
Bloomington, IN 47403
www.iuniverse.com
1-800-Authors (1-800-288-4677)

ISBN: 978-1-4401-9441-2 (sc)
ISBN: 978-1-4401-9442-9 (ebk)

Library of Congress Control Number: 2011904432

Printed in the United States of America

iUniverse rev. date: 04/01/2011

To Binish Bhagwanee, who loves chocolates, pizza, and me

~Zeeshan-ul-hassan Usmani

To all survivors of suicide bombing attacks

~Daniel R. Kirk

Table of Contents

Preface

Hardly a day passes without a television or newspaper story about a horrific suicide bombing. On average, a politically or religiously motivated attack takes place every six days somewhere in the world and the impacts are often devastating for the families and communities involved. Although suicide bombings account for only 3% of the terrorist attacks around the world, they claim 48% of the total deaths. Between 2004 and 2009 there were almost 700 bombing incidents in Iraq and 200 in Pakistan alone.

In early 2006, my doctoral student and Fulbright scholar, Zeeshan-ul-hassan Usmani, and I began to address the significant lack of modeling capability to simulate and reconstruct suicide bombing events. My expertise was in modeling and simulation of blast-induced traumatic brain injury, and Zeeshan was a talented and motivated computer scientist from Pakistan. We felt that if an advanced computer simulation tool was created to model suicide bombing events it could be used to save lives through better disaster management, triage of patients, and emergency resource allocation. This book is a result of our collaborative efforts to develop such a tool.

The comprehensive simulation platform we developed to model suicide bombing events is the first of its kind, and also includes comparisons of the results of our simulations against a database of past suicide bombing events in Pakistan. The simulation tool, called *BlastSim*, takes into account factors such as crowd pattern, density, shielding and demographics, geography and landscape in which the attack takes place, as well as details regarding the bomb, such as explosive energy content, overpressure and phase decay behavior of the explosive material and the shrapnel and fragment damage which may occur. The tool makes use of and compares an array of well-documented explosive and injury models, which are intelligently applied to various scenarios. The results of the various model combinations are then correlated against a statistical database. BlastSim allows the user to develop optimized crowd patterns to minimize the impact of a potential suicide bomber, study model sensitivity to any input/control parameter, and plan for emergency medical action strategies. The simulation can also be used to re-create the bombing event for forensic analyses. Furthermore, the tool also has the capability to calculate the economic impact of a bombing in various locations around the world including potential impact to gross domestic product and cost to the government to take care of injured individuals.

The work presented in the volume is multidisciplinary in its nature and includes modeling and simulation (platform for tool development), computational physics (simulation of blast-waves and pulse duration, dynamics of explosives in open and confined spaces), computational geometry (partial and full blockers within a crowd, smart rendering of scenes), computer graphics (modeling of virtual crowds), psychology (mob behavior, diffusion of rumors and stampede), and economics (cost impact of a bombing event).

The BlastSim can predict the number of dead and injured in a suicide bombing incident with 87% accuracy. Line-of-sight with an attacker, rushing towards an exit, announcing the threat of a suicide bombing, sitting inside a vehicle or building, and standing closer to a wall or a rigid surface were found to be the most lethal choices both during and after an attack. The findings can have implications for emergency response and counter terrorism.

The BlastSim tool has attracted the interest of numerous agencies such as the Federal Bureau of Investigation, the Army, the Department of Defense, the National Security Agency, as well as agencies from other countries. Finally it is our sincere hope that this research will continue to provide further motivation, direction, and interest from academia, government, and industry to investigate suicide bombing attacks in hopes of making the world a safer place.

Daniel R. Kirk, Ph.D.
Florida Institute of Technology
November 2009

Acknowledgments

"If the only prayer you ever say in your entire
life is 'thank you', it will be enough."

~Meister Eckhart

Words alone cannot adequately express our sincere gratitude to all those who facilitated and encouraged the development of this work.

Foremost we would like to acknowledge and thank the Fulbright Commission for their comprehensive support of this project through doctoral tuition, stipends, and travel funds. We are also indebted to a number of individuals at the Florida Institute of Technology, where this research was performed. Many thanks to professors Dr. Philip Bernhard, Dr. Ryan Stansifer, and Dr. Héctor Gutiérrez for their invaluable comments and to Provost T. Dwayne McCay for his support and encouragement. We would also like to thank department heads Dr. William Shoaff, of computer science, and Dr. Pei-feng Hsu, of mechanical and aerospace engineering for their support and co-operation in this inter-disciplinary pursuit.

Special thanks to Dr. Omer Salahuddin and Dr. Nasir A. Malik from POF hospital Wah-Cantt, Asad Khizar Malik from King Edward Medical University, and Asif and Arif Surani from Dow Medical College for helping us collect suicide bombing victims' data and to Ayaz Khan of Federal Intelligence Agency (FIA) of Pakistan for providing the pertinent details of bombing incidents. The benchmarking of our models against real-life situations, which is so critical to this type of study, would not have been possible without your contributions to our project. We are also indebted to Bill and Lane Anderson for proofreading this manuscript.

Finally, we wish to recognize the most important individuals of all – the survivors, families and friends who have had their worlds torn apart because of suicide bombings; we acknowledge your courage and fortitude.

Zeeshan-ul-hassan Usmani, Ph.D.
zusmani@my.fit.edu

Daniel R. Kirk, Ph.D.
dkirk@fit.edu

Florida Institute of Technology
November 2009

1. Introduction

"We could not stay there and run the risk of
another suicide attack on our Marines"
 ~ Ronald Reagan, *An American Life*

Gunpowder made its debut in the mid 800s [Thurman 2006] and has undergone enormous changes in its manufacturing and use in the last twelve and a half centuries. Unfortunately, the application of explosives transitioned from mining and constructive uses to destructive and lethal applications. Humans have experimented with chemical explosives for centuries to make them more lethal, and thus gain control and power. Over the course of a dozen centuries, explosives technology has become widely accessible to members of the public. Simple but effective Improvised Explosive Devices (IED) can be quickly assembled in a garage and are able to claim the lives of a few dozen people in a typical suicide bombing attack.

Suicide bombing is an *"operational method in which the very act of the attack is dependent upon the death of the perpetrator"* [Ganor 2001]. A suicide attack can be defined as a politically motivated and violent-intended action, with prior intent, by one or more individuals who choose to take their own life while causing maximum damage to the chosen target. Suicide bombing has become one of the most lethal, unpredictable and favorite modus operandi of terrorist organizations. Though only 3% of all terrorist attacks around the world can be classified as suicide bombing attacks, these account for 48% of the casualties [Pape 2005]. The average number of deaths per incident for suicide bombing attacks was 13 over the period of 1980 to 2001 (excluding 9/11). This number is far above the average of less than one death per incident across all types of terrorism attacks over the

1

same time period [Harrison 2004]. In Israel, the average number of deaths per incident was 31.4 over the period of November 2000 to November 2003 [Harrison 2006]. The average number of deaths in Pakistan was 14.2 over the period of 2006 and 2007 [Usmani and Kirk 2009].

The world is full of unwanted explosives, brutal bombings, accidents, and violent conflicts, and there is a need to understand the impacts of these explosions on ones surroundings, the environment and most important on human bodies. There is a growing need and interest in treating explosion-related injuries in emergency rooms, a phenomenon traditionally only considered to be present in the emergency units of battlefields. Suicide bombers, unlike any other device or means of destruction, can think and therefore detonate a charge at an optimal location, with perfect timing to cause maximum carnage and destruction. Suicide bombers are adaptive, and can quickly change targets if forced by security risk or the availability of better targets. Suicide attacks are relatively inexpensive to fund and technologically primitive, work most of the time, and require no escape plan [FEMA, 2004].

1.1. Background and Motivation for this Book

There is a growing trend of bombings and explosive use in the United States and in civilian settings. 81% of bombings in 2001 throughout the world happened in civilian sites [David 2008]. In 2001, 74% of the terrorist attacks were against the U.S. facilities around the world with an average of one attack per day [David 2008]. The U.S. produces 5 billion pounds of legally made commercial explosives each year. According to the FBI, there were 17,579 criminal bombings in the U.S. between 1988-1997 with an average of 5 bombings per day that claimed 830 deaths and 4063 injuries, which is higher than any other disaster in the same time period – hurricane, lightning, earthquake etc. [David 2008]. There were 214 bombings on the U.S. embassies worldwide with an average of 2 bombings per country, and 86% of all terrorist incidents in the U.S. have been bombings [David 2008].

The trend is parallel in other countries with U.S. involvement. One of the reasons behind the growth of such attacks is that historically suicide bombing attacks have forced states to change their decisions. For example, the U.S. left Lebanon in 1983 after a marine barracks bombing. Israel followed in 1985 after more than 800 deaths. Similarly, Spain left Iraq after the Madrid bombings in March 2004 [David 2008]. Over the last 5 years, the U.S. Department of Defense spent more than $13 billion on counter-IED technologies and efforts [Zorpette 2008].

Past research has focused on developing psychological profiles of suicide bombers [Lester, Yang, and Lindsay 2004], understanding the economic logic behind the attacks [Gupta and Mundra 2005, Harrison 2004, Harrison 2006], explaining the strategic and political gains of these attacks, their role in destabilizing countries [Azam 2005, Ganor 2000], and the role of bystanders in reducing casualties [Kress, 2004, Harrison 2006]. There is also an enormous amount of data in the military domain about explosions and their impact on structures and individuals, however, it is less helpful when measuring the detriment of suicide bombing attacks on military personnel because they are in the best shape and health, wearing personal protection gear, have access to highly sophisticated medical care, and the perpetrator typically uses commercial explosives with high tech shrapnel and controlled detonation. In contrast, in civilian settings there is a more diverse population with elderly and children, with pre-existing medical conditions, wearing no protection gear, surrounded by vulnerable buildings and structures, less or no immediate medical care, and perpetrators are novices with homemade explosives, and nuts, bolts and screws as shrapnel.

With current knowledge about explosives (e.g., mathematical models, pulse duration, peak overpressure ratios, medical records of victims, etc) and recent advances in computational fluid dynamics, one should be able to create a realistic simulation model to measure the effects of an explosive blast on humans and make recommendations to mitigate the effects. The risk can be reduced by analyzing the relationship between blasts and exposed individuals. Chapter 2 of this book presents current state-of-the-art explosion modeling in support of these goals. These models can help in risk assessment, and when designing or assessing features (e.g., enhanced structural loading capability, helmets, body armor, etc) to mitigate blast effects. The most complex models have the capability to apply to diverse situations, but require extensive time and computational resources. On the other hand, simple models are fast, but often rely on one-dimensional rough approximations of physical properties and scenario geometry.

The goal of the work is to predict the magnitude of injuries and lethality on humans from a blast-wave with various explosive and crowd characteristics, and to compare, contrast, and analyze the performance of explosive and injury models against the real-life data of suicide bombing incidents. The proposed simulation BlastSim is capable of assessing the impact of crowd formation patterns, crowd density, and a blast's initial conditions on the magnitude of injury and number of casualties during a suicide bombing attack. It also examines variables such as the number and arrangement of people within a crowd for typical layouts, the number of suicide bombers, and the nature of the explosion, including equivalent weight of TNT, the duration of the resulting blast wave pulse, and the type and amount of shrapnel used. The work also explains the physics, explosive models, mathematics and the assumptions one needs to create such a simulation. Furthermore, it describes human shields available in the crowd with partial and full coverage. The simulation can also be used to re-create the unfortunate event for forensic footprints and analysis. As a computer scientist, our interest in this study is utilitarian – we are interested in applications of these models rather than theoretical discussion on fundamentals of blast physics.

This inter-disciplinary research touches the domains of Modeling and Simulation (platform for the experiments), Computational Physics (dynamics of explosives in open and confined spaces), Computational Geometry (partial and full blockers, smart rendering of scenes), Aerospace and Mechanical Engineering (simulation of blast-waves and pulse duration, Computational Fluid Dynamics), Computer Graphics (modeling of virtual crowds), and Psychology (Mob Behavior, Rumors and Stampede). There are numerous applications for this simulation, it can be used to predict the levels of injuries to humans, re-create the suicide bombing event for forensics analysis, can help in event planning, emergency response and risk assessment of vulnerable scenarios.

1.2. Scope, Objectives and Organization

The main objective of explosion modeling with various crowd topologies is to determine the relationship between the explosion initial conditions and exposed individuals. By analyzing this relationship, it is likely to establish a more comprehensive understanding of ways to mitigate the effects of a suicide bomber attack, reduce the risks or re-create an event. The goals of this work are to:

1. Predict blast injuries as a function of explosion properties, crowd characteristics and injury model.
2. Recommend optimal crowd formations to reduce injuries and increase accessibility of emergency response teams.
3. Reconstruct a suicide bombing event with given crowd and explosive characteristics for forensic analysis.
4. Develop an easy-to-use simulation tool that can be used by scientists, researchers, doctors and government officials to incorporate quickly and understand a suicide bombing event.

The model will be benchmarked by a three-tier validation process:

1. The simulation results will be compared against existing explosion models (Harold Brode, Kingrey Bulmash, Kinney and Gilbert, Paul Cooper, J. Clutter etc,).
2. The results will be compared and contrasted with semi-empirical injury prediction models (Yang Wang Yu, Charles Stewart, Bowen's Lethality Curves etc,).
3. The results will be compared and fine-tuned against a benchmark database of real-life incidents, e.g., data from 189 suicide bombing incidents in Pakistan which occurred between 2000 and 2009.

The work is, however, not intended to address secondary and tertiary injuries such as those due to fire or structural collapse, triage of emergency management, complex blast wave inside a vehicle or building, underwater explosions or impact of landmines. The work is restricted to the number of deaths and severity of injuries to a crowd after a suicide bombing explosion. There is no scientific evidence that our results can be scaled and extended to confined or underwater explosions.

The book is divided into the following chapters: Chapter 1 introduces the concept of suicide bombing and explosions, motivations and background, research scope, objectives and limits of the study. Chapter 2 provides a comprehensive literature review on existing software and models on explosion modeling and blast waves. The chapter ends with a summary of missing components and future areas of research. Chapter 3 describes the explosion models used in this work with examples, and it also explains the methodology of their use. Chapter 4 explores the domain of blast injury to humans, available models from the literature and mapping of overpressure PSI (pounds-per-square-inch) to the severity of injury. It also discusses the role and impact of fragmentation and shrapnel in explosions and suicide bombings. Chapter 5 delves into the details of partial and full blockage by other humans in two and three-dimensional environments. Chapter 6 introduces the suicide bombing database of actual events that took place in Pakistan between 2004 and 2009. Chapter 7 presents the BlastSim simulator, modeling approach, and various sections and working of the software. Chapter 8 conveys the final results and their analysis. The book concludes at Chapter 9 with a research summary and future direction.

2. State-of-the-Art in Explosion Modeling

"The solution to the problem changes the problem"

~ Peer's Law

The goals of this chapter is to review the state-of-the-art in explosion modeling and simulation, identify the relative strengths and weaknesses of current analytical and numerical models, and classify them into different categories of utility and to identify future research directions. The main objective of explosion modeling is to determine the relationship between blast wave parameters and exposed individuals and structures. By analyzing this relationship, a more complete understanding of methods to mitigate the highly deleterious effects of an explosion may be identified. Explosion modeling requires the knowledge of physical parameters of explosions (i.e. peak overpressure, duration, and impulse), projectiles, fragmentation and debris, chemical properties of explosive materials, complex details of simulating gaseous and combustion flows with boundary conditions, application of advanced computational fluid dynamics to model details of the blast-target interaction and the overall impact of explosions on humans and structures, as benchmarked by experimental and theoretical studies. Seventeen explosion modeling tools have been reviewed and categorized based on their theoretical foundations and applicability. This chapter also suggests a comprehensive matrix for model comparison, and concludes with a discussion of promising future research directions.

The models differ based on their complexity to represent underlying blast physics, geometrical representations of scenarios and blockage ratios [Abdel-Gayed 1987, Freeman 1994, Hjertager 1982, Krauthammer 2008, Newmark 1979, Mercx 1993, Pritchard *et al.* 1999]. The models can help in risk assessments, and when designing or assessing features (enhanced structural loading capability, helmets, body armor etc) to mitigate blast effects. The most complex models can be applied to diverse situations but require extensive time and computational resources. On the other hand, simple, analytical models are fast, but often rely on one-dimensional approximations of physical properties and scenario geometry.

The effects of an explosion are contingent upon various factors [Roe 1981]:

- explosive type (i.e. TNT, RDX, C4, AN etc.)
- explosive weight (pounds)
- explosive overpressure PSI
- ignition source and criteria
- crowd density (number of people per square meter)
- crowd demographics (i.e. age, gender, weight, height)
- pulse duration (milliseconds), and reflection waves
- blockage ratios (percentage)
- size, shape, location, and number of obstacles
- projectiles, debris and fragments
- shape of the explosive carrier

This literature survey focused primarily on research papers, books and articles dealing with blast wave analysis (empirical and theoretical), modeling and simulation, and its effects on structures in general, and on humans in particular. A good amount of work on blast waves and explosives is available in the public domain. However, more detailed and complex descriptions of different explosives and their behavior when interacting with buildings and humans are still restricted due to military significance and applications. In addition, a number of articles related to the computational aspects of blast wave modeling were also reviewed.

This literature review was conducted in two broad thrusts. First, papers and books on blast waves and explosion models were reviewed. While there are hundreds of articles covering the research developed in the last five decades on the physics of blast waves and explosions, the actual mathematical formulation has not varied significantly. The second thrust was in identifying advanced computational models, assessment methods and explosion models in risk management and emergency response. The majority of the articles reviewed used some combination of both areas. In this chapter, however, the author has categorized the papers based on their primary objectives.

There are two parts of this section. The first part explains the categories of explosion and blast wave models followed by a brief description of well-known and most commonly used models/tools in each category. The second part introduces an A-to-Z matrix for comparison and analysis of these models, followed by a summary of the findings.

2.1. Explosion Models and Simulations

There are primarily three kinds of models available for the simulation and assessment of explosions and blast waves: empirical or co-relation models, phenomenological or physical models and computational fluid dynamics (CFD) or numerical models. The models are different on the basis of geometry, explosive types, mechanics of blast waves and blockage being used. Empirical models are based on previous field experimental data and try to "fit" new situations to the previously observed data by using scaling laws. The phenomenological models make rough approximations of given geometries, and contain advanced physics capabilities. The CFD models use sub-grid and unstructured models to represent objects in a given geometry. Table 2.1 provides references of representative work in each category.

Table 2.1: Categorization of explosion models

Approach	Representative Work
Empirical	• TNT Equivalence [Bjerketvedt, Bakke and Wingerden 1997, Gilbert and Keneth 1985, Pritchard 1989] • TNO [Mercx and Berg 1997, Wiekema 1980, Pritchard 1999] • Multi-Energy [Berg 1985, Mercx 1993, Pritchard 1989]

Approach	Representative Work
Empirical (cont.)	• Baker Strehlow [Baker *et al.* 1994, Strehlow and Baker 1976] Congestion Assessment Method [Mercx and Berg 1997, Puttock 1995, Puttock 1999, Puttock, Yardley, and Cresswell 2000] • Sedgwick Assessment Loss Method [Thyer 1997] • Blast/FX [Fertal and Leone 2000, Serge and Comton 2005]
Phenomenological	• Shell Code for Overpressure Prediction in gas Explosions [Cates and Samuels 1991, Puttock *et al.* 1996] • Confined Linked Chamber Explosion [Abdel-Gayed 1987, Bray 1990, Bray, Libby, and Moss 1985, Catlin and Lindstedt 1991, Catlin, Fairweather, and Ibrahim 1995, Chippett 1984, Fairweather *et al.* 1996, Strehlow *et al.* 1979]
CFD and/or Numerical	• EXSIM [Hjertager 1982, Patankar and Spalding 1972] • Flame Acceleration Simulator [Arntzen 1995, Arntzen 1998, Leer 1982, Leer 1974, Selby and Burgan 1998, Wingerden 2001] • AutoReaGas [Bray 1990, Lea 2008] • CFX-4 [Pritchard 1989, Pritchard *et al.* 1999] • COBRA [Catlin, Fairweather, and Ibrahim 1995, Godunov 1959, Jones 1980, Popat *et al.* 1996, Catlin *et al.* 1995] • Imperial College Research Code [Bray, Champion, and Libby 1989, Hulek and Lindstedt 1996, Lindstedt and Váos 1998, Lindstedt, Hulek, and Vaos 1997, Puttock, Yardley, and Cresswell 2000] • NEWT [Birkby, Cant, and Savill 1997, Bray 1977, Freeman 1994, Puttock 1995, Watterson *et al.* 1996, Watterson *et al.* 1998] • REACFLOW [Arienti, Huld, and Wilkening 1998, Wilkening and Huld 1999]

The following paragraphs present basic definitions, capabilities and limitations of currently available models in all three categories.

2.1.1. Empirical/Co-relation Models

Empirical models are based on the analysis of experimental data correlation. The models use scaling laws to project pressure-distance and pressure-time curves for a given explosion with specified weight and pulse durations. In principle, these models involve less representation of underlying physics relative to the other categories and have no considerations for geometry. Following is a list of the empirical models that are most commonly used in industry and other civil settings for risk assessment.

1. **TNT Equivalence:** TNT equivalence is a method of quantifying the energy released in explosions [Bjerketvedt 1997]. The model has been used extensively to predict peak pressures from TNT mass. The model uses pressure-distance curves to yield the peak pressure. From landmines to suicide bombing and from industrial accidents to nuclear explosions, TNT is used as a yardstick of measurement. This model is easier to understand and is the benchmark for other experiments [Gilbert and Kenneth 1985]. Weak explosions are not well represented in this model. It only provides the information for the positive phase duration and overestimates near-field outcomes. [Pritchard 1989]

2. **TNO:** The TNO method assumes that the whole vapor cloud contributes to the overpressure, rather than just the portion which happens to be in a confined or congested area [Mercx and Berg 1997]. The TNO method is now considered obsolete, and has been replaced by the Multi-Energy method [Berg 1985, Pritchard 1989]

3. **Multi-Energy:** The Multi-Energy model is based on the observation that overpressure increases with confinement [Berg 1985]. In general, there will be more overpressure in a confined area compare to an open-space. This model was proposed by Berg Van Den [Mercx 1993] and can be used to estimate the blast from gas explosions with variable strength. The model can be used to

read a non-dimensional "side-on" overpressure and positive phase duration from diagrams, where the source strength is represented by a set of curves. It is a fast method but not ideal for weak explosions [Berg 1985]. The model is incapable of dealing with congested regions, complex geometries and multiple blast waves [Lea 2004, Pritchard 1989]

4. **Baker-Strehlow:** The Baker-Strehlow method was the result of hazards assessments in industrial settings based on a comprehensive examination of potential explosion sites, dimensionality of confined areas (to work out flame speed) and the calculation of burning velocity of fuel mixtures [Baker and Doolittle 1998]. The impulse duration and blast pressure can be read from a series of graphs based on numerical simulations [Strehlow *et al.* 1979]. This model is easy to use, fast and can work with multiple geometries and confinements, as well as with multiple sources of explosions.

5. **Congestion Assessment Method (CAM):** The Congestion Assessment Method (CAM) was developed at the Shell Thornton Research Center as a result of the Modeling and Experimental Research into Gas Explosions (MERGE) project [Mercx and Berg 1997, Puttock 1995]. The model is based on a decision tree procedure to estimate the source pressure with respect to plant layout (e.g., degree of confinement, congestion and type of fuel involved) [Puttock 1999]. The method was designed to yield conservative pressures. The methods can be divided into three steps: *Assessment* – where an assessment of the region is carried out to assign the reference pressure (*Pref*), which is the maximum overpressure generated by deflagration; *Type of Explosion* – determined by equivalent factor; and *Estimation* – In this step the pressure experienced at various distances from the source of an explosion is estimated [Puttock, Yardley, and Cresswell 2000]. The model has been enhanced and further extended by Puttock [Puttock, Yardley, and Cresswell 2000]. It is easy to use, fast to run and is calibrated against a large number of experiments. This model can also handle asymmetrical congestion. Geometries are roughly represented in this model.

6. **Sedgwick Assessment Loss Method (SALM):** The SALM model is a refinement of the CAM model discussed above. Thyer tested the vapor cloud explosion (VCE) model developed by Sedgwick Energy Ltd [Baker 1994, Thyer 1997]. He noted that it is hard to replicate the CAM method for other geometries and plants, and he developed a GUI based tool to represent the plant with different geometries and architectures [Tang *et al.* 1994]. It is easy to use and produces results fast, however, complex geometries are not well represented [Thyer 1997].

7. **Blast/FX:** Blast/FX explosive effects analysis software was developed by Northrop Grumman for the Federal Aviation Agency (FAA) [Fertal and Leone 2000, Serge 2005]. Blast/FX is based on the empirical TNT equivalence method and has an advance GUI interface developed in C++. Users can quickly create a representation of a scenario with walls, glasses, population set, explosive device characteristics (like weight, type and fragments) to get results such as blast overpressure from any location relative to the source of an explosion. Probabilities of casualties and human injury damage due to fragment penetrations can also be calculated. There are four basic modes of scenario implementation in Blast/FX: beams, columns, floors, and walls. The software uses standard specifications for most of the components (like glass, steel reinforcement and columns) from the American Institute of Steel Construction (AISC) standard [Fertal and Leone 2000]. A user can also define custom-made material for the building and walls. One of the prime advantages that differentiate this model from other empirical models and software is the ability to select different types of explosives with different charge loads. However, the software still fails to model blockage and its impact, negative phase and reflection waves and does not work for open space scenarios.

2.1.2. Phenomenological/Physical Models

Phenomenological models are usually better than empirical models, because they represent only the essential physics of explosions and use modeled geometry [Lea 2004]. These models make no attempt to simulate the given geometry scenario; instead, the geometries are represented by an idealized form. This simplification has less effect on off-shore simulations with free-field scenarios, but proves risky and quite misleading with complex geometries, on-shore plants and with multiple obstacles [Lea 2004]. Following are the two most commonly used phenomenological models:

1. **Shell Code for Overpressure Prediction in gas Explosions (SCOPE):** SCOPE was the first phenomenological model designed for offshore explosion modeling. The development was done at Shell's Thornton Research Centre [Cates 1991]. The model can be applied to any geometry with a single flame path. Subsequently, SCOPE 2 was introduced based on work by Caste and Samuel. Shell launched SCOPE 3 in 1994 [Puttock, Yardley and Cresswell 2000]. SCOPE models the basic essential physics of explosions. It is a one-dimensional model and based on idealized geometry containing a series of obstacles. The flow through each obstacle determines the turbulence [Puttock, Yardley and Cresswell 2000]. SCOPE is somewhere between empirical models that basically fit the models to experimental data and CFD, which models complex details of flows and combustion. SCOPE 3 is the only model that considers mixed objects or partial blockage among obstacles. It can handle venting and external explosions, with limits to flame acceleration and speed. It has been validated against a large number of small, medium, and large scale experiments [Cates 1991]. The model is limited however, in that it deals with single enclosures and has less complex geometric specifications.

2. **Confined LInked CHamber Explosion (CLICHÉ):** CLICHÉ was developed by Advantica Technologies [Abdel-Gayed 1987]. Originally developed to study confined explosions in buildings, its use has been extended to model off-and-on-shore explosions [Bray 1990]. CLICHE is based on the research of Catlin *et al* and Chippet. [Catlin, Fairweather, and Ibrahim 1995, Chippet 1984]. This work is useful mainly for plants with semi-confined multiple chambers (i.e. pipes and process vessels).

The model incorporates resistance and the loss of pressure among chambers, from confined to semi-confined spaces [Bray and Moss 1977]. Parameters to the model include drag and flame/obstacle interaction, which are determined from a numerical database containing a detailed description of plant geometry [Strehlow and Baker 1976]. Furthermore, the model uses two combustion models for internal and external combustions to determine both laminar and turbulent burning velocities [Chippett 1984]. CLICHÉ uses conservation laws for the un-burnt and burnt gas volumes in each chamber to predict the explosion effects and pressure [Fairweather and Vasey 1982]. It is a simple model based on fundamental physics and empirical correlations. The model can also generate its own input parameters from the obstacles database.

2.1.3. CFD/Numerical Models

Computational Fluid Dynamics (CFD) models find numerical solutions to partial differential equations governing the explosion process. CFD is one of the branches of fluid mechanics that employs numerical methods to solve problems dealing with fluid dynamics and flows. These models are, in general, time and resource consuming. There are dozens of methods that have been proposed to approximate situations, geometries and their underlying specifications. The numerical solutions are achieved through discretization of the solution domain in both space and time. CFD solutions contain a wealth of information from pressure, flow behaviors, velocities, density, decay, concentrations, refractions, impulse and negative phase. However, it is very important that the models used for analysis should also be calibrated against controlled and well-defined experimental results that can be repeated. CFD results should be considered as a complementary means of investigation, due to the high risk of improper modeling and numerical inaccuracy resulting from the hardware and software being used. Following is a selection of widely used CFD models in industry, academia and military settings.

1. **EXSIM:** EXSIM was developed at the Telemark Technological R&D Centre (Tel-Tek) in Norway [Hjertager 1982], and at the

Shell Global Solutions of the United Kingdom [Puttock 1999]. EXSIM is a structured Cartesian grid, semi-implicit, finite volume model that relies on the Porosity / Distributed Resistance (PDR) method for the representation of small-scale objects [Hjertager 1982]. The model has been validated against small-scale, medium-scale and large-scale experiments [Hjertager 1982]. The model can work on congested, but unconfined geometries and can handle external explosions [Puttock 1999]. The model is also able to integrate with CAD data.

2. **FLame ACceleration Simulator (FLACS):** FLACS was developed by the Christian Michelsen Research Institute (now CMR-GEXCON) in Norway [Arntzen 1995, Arntzen 1998]. FLACS is a finite volume model based on a structured Cartesian grid [Arntzen 1995]. The Porosity / Distributed Resistance approach is used to model sub-grid scale obstacles [Selby 1998]. The model has been validated against large scale experiments and can handle congested and multiple geometries [Leer 1974]. The model incorporates external explosions and can integrate CAD data [Wingerden 2001]. The model is also scalable to underwater explosions [Leer 1974]. However, the model does not allow grid refinements.

3. **AutoReaGas:** AutoReaGas combines features of the REAGAS and BLAST models developed by TNO and then transformed into an interactive environment based on the AUTODYN-3D model developed by Century Dynamics Ltd [Bray 1990]. REAGAS is a gas explosion simulator, whereas BLAST simulates the propagation of the blast waves [Lea 2004]. The REAGAS works as the gas explosion solver while the BLAST works as a blast solver in AutoReaGas. The model has been validated against large experiments and can use CAD data. The model can accept a large number of objects through dynamic memory allocation of the objects database. However it does requires a heavy setup to run, like highly sophisticated computer servers with an enormous speed and memory.

4. **CFX-4:** CFX-4 was developed by AEA Technology Engineering Software at Harwell, UK [Pritchard, Freeman, and Guilbert 1996]. It is a general purpose, structured-grid, finite volume, commercially available CFD model [Pritchard *et al.* 1999]. CFX-4 allows multi-block, non-orthogonal grids for complex geometries. A newer version, CFX-5 has an unstructured grid, but lacks the basic physical models to simulate an explosion. CFX-4 also includes a full Reynolds stress turbulence model and a multi-block capability for greater control over meshing. The model has wide selection of discretization schemes and a number of turbulence models. It can also integrate with CAD data and has an integrated geometry building front-end [Pritchard, Freeman, and Guilbert 1996]. The model, however, is only tuned for methane and hydrogen explosions, and uses a thin flame model which is not well suited to explosion modeling [Pritchard *et al.* 1999]. The explosion and ignition models used in this model have not been thoroughly validated.

5. **COBRA:** COBRA was developed by Mantis Numerics in conjunction with Advantica Technologies [Catlin, Fairweather, and Ibrahim 1995]. COBRA uses an explicit (or implicit) second order accurate (spatial and temporal), finite-volume integration scheme with an adaptive grid algorithm [Fairweather *et al.* 1999]. COBRA usually works with MUVI [Godunov 1959], another simple visualization tool by the same company. The newer version PICA is much faster than COBRA [Fairweather *et al.* 1999]. It uses a Cartesian mesh, which makes meshing particularly easy, but can also handle cylindrical polar or arbitrary hexahedral meshes. The model also uses advanced grid refinement that enables flame front tracking and shock wave capturing. It can also read CAD generated geometries [Popat 1996, Catlin and Lindstedt 1991]. The model is time consuming, however, and the setting of complex geometries is almost impossible. In addition, visualization of flow fields with the MUVI is slow and laborious compared to commercially available visualization tools, i.e. EnSight and Fieldview [Jones 1980]

6. **Imperial College Research Model:** This model was developed by Lindstedt [Bray 1990] and incorporates all the latest findings with respect to a combustion model, a sophisticated gradient/flame front tracking refinement and a refinement mesh algorithm [Hulek and Lindstedt 1996]. The model uses adaptive meshing capability and detail chemistry kinetics, and can run in parallel [Puttock, Yardley, and Cresswell 2000]. Unfortunately, it is very slow and consumes too much computing power [Hulek and Lindstedt 1996]. The model is not readily available.

7. **NEWT:** NEWT is a finite volume, unstructured, three dimensional, CFD model with an adaptive mesh [Birkby, Cant, and Savill 1997]. The adaptive mesh can be tailored for complex geometries. NEWT is currently being used for explosion effects prediction in the Engineering Department of Cambridge University [Bray, Champion, and Libby 1989]. It can predict the explosion effects with hundreds of obstacles [Puttock, Yardley, and Cresswell 2000]. The model uses an adaptive mesh algorithm and unstructured meshes, which reduces the amount of effort required to generate a mesh [Watterson *et al.* 1996]. It supports complex geometries, and any 3D tetrahedral mesh generator can be used with the format expected by NEWT [Watterson *et al.* 1998].

8. **REACFLOW:** This model was developed by the Joint Research Centre of the European Union in Ispra, Italy [Arienti, Huld, and Wilkening 1998, Leer 1974]. REACFLOW is an unstructured grid system with an adaptive mesh that can represent 2D and 3D geometries [Wilkening and Hudd 1999]. The system breaks down objects into elements like triangular 2-D and tetrahedral 3-D [Wilkening and Huss 1999]. It uses unstructured mesh capability for easier meshing and adaptive meshing for better obstacle representation.

2.2. A-to-Z Comparison Matrix

Based on the aforementioned requirements of a good model, and the observed characteristics of the existing models, an A-to-Z matrix is presented for model comparison. This matrix reveals capabilities, limitations, and also provides an overall picture of the current state of the art in explosion modeling. Table 2.2 explains the criterion and parameters used for testing and comparison of these models and Table 2.3 illustrates the results.

Table 2.2. A-to-Z Matrix for Model Comparison and Evaluation

Abbreviation	Criteria	Description
A	Approach	Category of Model (E = Empirical, P = Phenomenological, C = CFD)
B	Blockage and Obstacles	Does this model consider living and non-living blockages? E.g., Humans, Cars, Plants.
C	Calibrated	Was this model benchmarked and calibrated against previous experiments and field data?
D	Density of Crowd	Does this model consider density and population of a crowd in the area?
E	Easy to Configure	Is it easy to setup and run the model?
F	Fast	Is this model fast enough to yield the results quickly?
G	Geometry and Confinements	Does this model consider complex geometries and confinements?
H	Human Data	Does this model incorporate any real-life human data?
I	Integration	Can this model be integrated with other models and advance software like CAD/CAM?
J	Junk and Debris	Does this model consider debris and fragments with blast waves?
K	Killed	Does this model give the probability of victim's death?
L	Less Laborious	Does this model consume lesser amount of computer and memory resources?
M	Multiple Sources of Explosions	Does this model consider multiple sources of explosions?
N	Negative Phase	Does this model consider the negative phase of blast waves?

Abbreviation	Criteria	Description
O	Overestimation	Does this model overestimate the pressure yields of near-field experiments?
P	Projectiles	Does this model consider projectiles?
Q	Quantity of Explosives	Can we give different weights/ quantities for explosives?
R	Reflection Waves	Does this model consider reflection waves?
S	Scalable	Is this model is scalable to multiple blast waves and underwater explosions?
T	Topology/Scenarios	Does this model consider various topologies and crowd formations?
U	Understandable	Is this model easy to understand?
V	Various Explosives	Does this model work with different types of explosives?
W	Weak Explosions	Can we represent weak explosions with this model?
X	X-Axis	Is it a one-dimensional model?
Y	Y-Axis	Is it a two-dimensional model?
Z	Z-Axis	Is it a three-dimensional model?

Overall there are two main limitations for empirical models: rough approximations of geometric representation and the relative lack of incorporated physics that have to be calibrated for each scenario and explosive type [Simmonds *et al.* 2001]. The assumptions made by the user for explosive strength and degree of confinement can lead to an array of possible answers or uncertainties. There are methods and criteria available for such assumptions, but the model employs the basic simplified approach to generate faster results with minimum efforts possible.

Once the assumptions and/or knowledge about explosive strength, confinement, density, and blockage have been identified, it is easy to calculate overpressure and pulse given distance and time. The empirical nature of these models gives confidence that the results are adequate as long as one is working with a good representation [Walter 2004]. However, different users can choose different parameter values and that can lead to different results.

Table 2.3. Model Comparison Results

Model	A	B	C	D	E	F	G	H	I	J	K	L	M	N	O	P	Q	R	S	T	U	V	W	X	Y	Z
TNT Equivalence	E		✓		✓	✓					✓	✓			✓		✓				✓	✓		✓	✓	
TNO	E		✓		✓	✓					✓	✓			✓		✓					✓		✓	✓	
Multi-Energy	E		✓			✓					✓	✓			✓		✓					✓		✓	✓	
Baker-Strehlow	E		✓		✓	✓					✓	✓	✓		✓		✓				✓			✓	✓	
CAM	E	✓	✓		✓	✓			✓		✓	✓			✓		✓							✓	✓	
SALM	E				✓	✓					✓	✓			✓		✓							✓	✓	
Blast/FX	E		✓		✓	✓	✓	✓		✓	✓	✓			✓	✓	✓	✓		✓	✓	✓		✓	✓	✓
SCOPE	P	✓	✓			✓					✓		✓		✓		✓					✓				
Cliché	P	✓	✓			✓					✓		✓		✓		✓							✓	✓	
Exsim	C		✓			✓	✓				✓	✓			✓									✓	✓	✓
FLACS	C		✓			✓	✓	✓			✓	✓			✓			✓						✓	✓	✓
AutoReaGas	C	✓	✓				✓				✓				✓									✓	✓	✓
CFX-4	C	✓				✓	✓	✓			✓				✓			✓						✓	✓	✓
COBRA	C		✓			✓	✓	✓			✓				✓					✓				✓	✓	✓
Imperial College	C					✓	✓	✓			✓	✓			✓									✓	✓	✓
NEWT	C	✓				✓	✓	✓			✓	✓			✓									✓	✓	✓
Reacflow	C	✓				✓	✓	✓			✓	✓			✓									✓	✓	✓

The majority of empirical models also tend to be overly conservative and do not provide good results for short distances. The empirical models provide very few details about overpressure and flow conditions, and produce incorrect results for mixture of explosives. Despite all of these shortcomings, empirical models are the most widely used models in industry and the military, mainly because of their ease of use, implementation, understanding and faster results. Several scenarios can be instantly tested with empirical models, and a user can then select a scenario for further investigation using advance models such as phenomenological and/or CFD.

The phenomenological models offer a good tradeoff when representing physical properties of an explosion without compromising too much on time and computing resources (as is the case with CFD models). The execution times for phenomenological models are short, on the order of a few seconds. These models are good for working on a large number of scenarios to get preliminary results, and then a user can choose a scenario to investigate further with CFD models. While the phenomenological models contain more physics than the empirical models, the geometry is still not well represented. There is also uncertainty introduced by non-unique obstacle representation. There have been a few improvements by researchers, for example, one of our studied models, CLICHÉ, calculates its input parameters from an obstacle database that allows a more accurate representation.

There are a few limitations as well when using the phenomenological models. Since the models are calibrated against medium and large scale experiments, they are only suitable for scenarios similar to the ones for which the models have been calibrated. For new scenarios and situations, experimental data is required to calibrate the new settings. These models can also be used in conjunction with empirical and CFD models, where there are a few uncertainties as well. For example, these models contain simplified geometrical descriptions that make it hard to accurately model complex situations and layouts. Furthermore, the phenomenological models disregard the presence of shock waves, hence the pressure distribution within a volume may be incorrectly predicted.

On the other hand, CFD is an important tool when used with the right geometry, initial and boundary conditions. It is, however, very hard to tune the parameters for each scenario and geometry. CFD models are time and resource consuming, usually taking a few days to run for a complex situation. The CFD models presented in Table 2 rely heavily on sub-models for representation, with simplified numerical equations for the solution of blast waves. The presented models of this category (except COBRA) allow an exact representation of explosion scenario geometry, only limited by computing power.

There are quite a few constraints for CFD models. The first constraint is the amount of memory for representing the modeled geometry. Researchers have suggested using parallel processors or cluster grids and partitioning the mesh into a number of smaller parts. Fitting all of the objects on the grid is another constraint that resulted in the development of techniques like the Porosity/Distributed Resistance (PDR) approach. PDR allows some form of geometric representation for large-scale scenarios but introduces uncertainties as well. Like phenomenological models, CFD models are also calibrated against medium and large scale experiments for certain scenarios, and work very well with scenarios similar to the ones for which the models have been calibrated. Another important limitation comes with the use of simple grids for a discrete computational domain. All of the CFD models present in Table 2 use Cartesian grids with sub-grid objects represented by the PDR. While it is easier to generate Cartesian meshes, even objects that are similar in size can be roughly represented. For example, a sphere can be represented by an equivalent cube on a Cartesian grid. This simplification can lead to uncertain performance.

CFD, in general, is a promising technology, but due to the heavy demand of computer memory and processing power, it is unlikely to be used for real complex geometries in the near future. It is possible to reduce the detailed kinetic schemes to a smaller set of species, but then the resulting set of species conversion equations will become mathematically inflexible and it will be hard to carry out the sensitivity analysis due to small changes in dependent variables.

2.3. Discussion and Future Directions

Significant progress has been made over the last two decades in the modeling and simulation of explosion and blast waves. However, it is clear from the survey that the capabilities and limitations of the majority of work follow the requirements in industry and non-civil settings. For example, none of the models considered open space scenarios like markets and streets. Another important parameter missed by almost all existing models is the plotting of multiple explosions, as witnessed in recent times [Usmani and Kirk 2009].

Most existing models have also neglected the effects of a blast wave's negative phase, reflection and refraction waves and blockage shields by living and non-living objects, crowd density considerations, projectiles and debris originating from explosive fragmentation, different explosive types and scenario visualization in 3D environments. Blast/FX is regarded by many as the best available explosion model for testing and evaluation of blast loading [Gilbert and Kenneth 1985], but it is based only on empirical studies with sheep and pigs. There is an acute need for an explosion effects model based on human data. While the models can provide some indication of blast damage and injury, collectively they have the following limitations:

1. Require too many computing resources for complex geometries and scenarios.
2. Require special hardware and software.
3. Require a subject matter expert to tune parameters for new situations.
4. Do not consider blockage and obstacles in three dimensional environments.
5. Lack the capability to work with different kinds of explosives.
6. Do not consider crowd formations, density and demographics.
7. Have no experimental data on humans.
8. Lack a direct mapping of overpressure to injuries on the human body.
9. Provide no capability to plug-in new equations and algorithms.
10. Provide no ability to assess changes in explosive characteristics.
11. Do not consider negative phase and reflection waves.

Resolution of these issues is needed for real-life risk assessment and emergency planning, and to develop a comprehensive model of a suicide bomber attack. The focus of this research is to address most (if not all) of these issues in order to develop an enhanced modeling and simulation capability.

3. Explosion Modeling for a Suicide Bombing Attack

"The blast wave is a shot without a bullet, a slash without a sword. It is present everywhere within its range."

~[Benzinger 1950]

This chapter presents the science of explosion modeling, including physics and types of an explosion, the TNT equivalence method, scaling laws, a set of blast overpressure prediction models and a section on blast forensics.

3.1. Physics of an Explosion

An *explosion* is a sudden release of energy that generates light, heat, noise and most importantly pressure, which results in a blast wave [Noon 2000]. Part of the energy is released as thermal radiation, and the other part is coupled into air (air- blast) and soil (ground-shock) as radially expanding shock waves [FEMA 2006]. A chemical explosion is caused by the energy released from a rapid chemical reaction. The chemical reaction may occur spontaneously (i.e., infinite rate kinetics approximation) or can be initiated by an ignition source (i.e., finite rate kinetics models) such as an electrical charge or flame [Palmer 2005]. Explosion that uses the ignition of flammable materials has higher chances of being accompanied by a high temperature fireball.

There are generally two types of explosions: deflagrating and detonating [Noon 2000].

- **Deflagrating Explosions:** are usually termed as slow and progressive burning explosives. The heat transfer usually depends on external factors like ambient pressure and temperature. These explosions move things around by pushing them from one side to another. In this case, high pressure gases coming from the source of the explosion impinges on surfaces with a lower side-on pressure. The resulting pressure differential yields enough net force to move the object around.

- **Detonating Explosions:** are characterized by high energy release, burn rate and peak overpressure. The energy dispersion is achieved by shock waves and stress, and do not necessarily depend on external factors like ambient pressure or temperature. Detonation explosions cause more local damage as compared to deflagrating explosions.

Explosions happen in very short time durations, typically in thousandths of a second (milliseconds). Gas generated by an explosion expands rapidly in every direction from the point of explosion. The rapidly expanding gas pushes the stationary gas in front of it, causing a region of high pressure known as a *blast wave* [Walter 2004]. This wave represents the *shock front* consisting of highly compressed air at overpressure much greater than in the region behind it [Oladitoye 1998]. The blast wave expands outwards at a very high velocity, oftentimes greater than the speed of sound (velocities range from 3,000 to 8,000 m per second). The blast wave loses energy quickly as its distance increases from the point of the explosion or epicenter [Dire 2007, Noon 2000, Irwin *et al.* 1999, FEMA 2006, Rogers 1959, Aizik *et al.* 2001]. The blast wave can be measured at any distance from the point of explosion [Abbasi and Khan 1998].

The difference between the blast wave pressure and the ambient air pressure is called the *overpressure* of the blast wave. Because the blast wave expands outwards so rapidly, behind the blast wave is a region of low air pressure. This low-pressure region "sucks" the air along with it, causing a wind that initially follows the blast wave, thus creating a *suction effect* [Oladitoye 1998]. As the blast wave continues outward, the relative pressure in front of, and behind the blast wave changes such that the direction of the wind can reverse direction, and for a time it can blow in towards the point of the explosion. This negative phase can move ten times slower than the positive pressure, since the speed of propagation depends on the pressure [Dire 2007]. Blast waves can damage rigid bodies in two ways. First it can rupture an object by creating a tensile stress within the object, and it can rotate or move the object by exerting force on its side [Martins, Buchanan, and Amanatides 2001].

The resulting pressure effect from an explosion damages organs in people and animals particularly at air-fluid interfaces. The wind propels fragments and people, causing penetrating or blunt injuries. The shock wave travelling outwards from the source is reflected when it meets objects with higher density than atmospheric pressure (i.e. ground) and travels back to the origin. The overpressure of the reflected wave may exceed the overpressure of the incident wave, and due to its higher velocity, will eventually catch up with the incident wave [Oladitoye 1998]. The resulting wave will travel horizontally and forms a single shock front know as *Mach front* or *Mach Stem.* The point where incident and reflected waves meet at some distance above the ground is usually referred as a *triple point* [Baker *et al.* 1983, Baker 1973].

A conventional bomb generates a blast wave that spreads out spherically from the origin of the explosion. Although the physics of blast waves are complex and nonlinear, a wave may be broadly characterized by its peak overpressure (pressure above atmospheric) and the duration of the positive phase of the blast event. Based on those two quantities, the intensity of the blast wave can be assessed and exposure threshold limits can be determined, although this only applies to a specific scenario. The biological response to the blast wave from conventional explosives depends predominantly on the peak overpressure and the duration of the positive phase [Dire 2007]. While the physical nature and source of explosions can vary greatly, the pressure-time profile of all blast waves have several critical features which are used to quantify the wave [Newmark 1979]. When the shock wave interacts with an object, reflection waves will be generated. The reflected pressure may be much higher than the incident pressure. The maximum impulse delivered is the area under the positive phase of the reflected pressure-time curve. Both the pressure and impulse (or duration time) are required to define the blast loading. Figure 3.1 depicts the overall mechanics of the blast wave defined in this section.

As an example, an explosion in a confined space with wave reflections and enhanced differences in pressure is shown in Figure 3.2. A blast wave inside a confined space will have repeated reflections from the interior surfaces that create a highly complex form. A complex blast wave is characterized by an incident blast wave, a jumble of reflected waves, and the static pressurization of the enclosure. The intensity and duration of a complex blast wave also depends on the volume of confinement and the available points of ventilation [Dire 2007].

Enhanced-blast explosive devices, in contrast, can have more damaging effects, and cause a greater proportion of blast injuries than conventional devices. In an enhanced-blast device, a primary blast disseminates the explosive and later triggers a secondary explosion. The high-pressure wave then radiates from a much larger area, prolonging the duration of the over-pressurization phase, thus increasing the total energy transmitted by the explosion. Depending on the type of explosive and the proximity to the target, the positive phase duration can vary between a few microseconds and several milliseconds [Gilbert and Kenneth 1985]

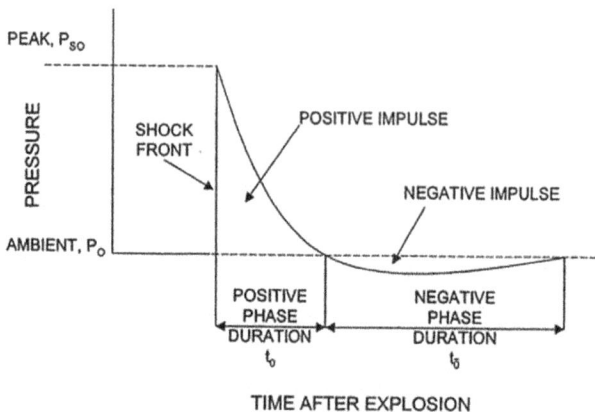

Figure 3.1. Blast wave showing positive and negative phase durations. Such waves may be characterized by the peak overpressure and durationof the positive phase [Ettouney 2001].

28

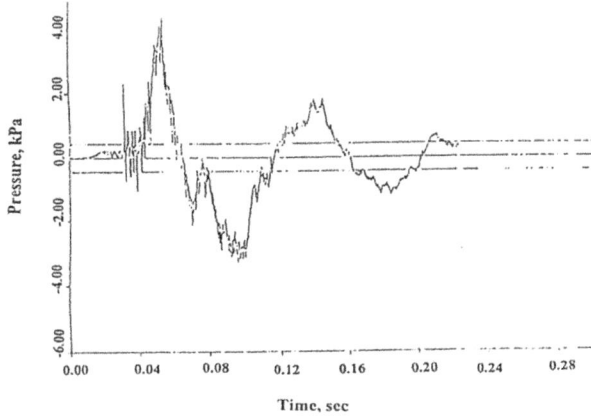

Figure 3.2. Pressure-time trace recorded behind a barrier after
firing a 155 mm shell. Complex wave forms result
from reflections and reverberations
[Johnson 2000].

Depending on the type of explosive, there may also be a fireball
associated with the explosion, which is produced during the initiating
chemical reactions. Most of the damage by an explosion to people, vehicles,
and structures, however, is done by the overpressure in the blast wave,
rather than by the fireball radius, which is confined relatively closely to
the blast origin. In contrast, the blast overpressure can be damaging over
distances of hundreds of initial blast diameters.

There are three kinds of blast overpressure [Dire 2007, Joachim *et al.*
1999]: *Static* – is the air compression in all directions due to the thermal
motion of the gas; *Dynamic* – is the force of moving particles at the edge of
the shockwave; and *Reflected* – pressure interacting with solid barriers and
pushed back due to intense compression of gas molecules. A reflected wave
can carry two to nine times' higher pressure than the original incident
peak pressure. A person who may be moderately injured in an explosion
can die, if he is standing next to the reflecting surface. It is important
to note the difference between static, dynamic and short-term dynamic
loads. Generally, static loads such as gravity do not produce inertia effects
and are not time dependent [Fertal and Leone 2000]. Dynamic loads, in

contrast oftentimes induced by earthquake or such things as wind gusts, are dependent on time (typically measured in tenth of seconds). Short term dynamic loads, like ones produced by explosions and debris, are non-oscillatory pulse loads which are measured in milliseconds [Fertal and Leone 2000].

Suicide bombers use improvised explosive devices (IEDs) to kill people and cause all the carnage and destruction they can. An IED comprises of two main components: an explosive charge, and a fusing system. An explosive charge can be anything from commercially available TNT to homemade chemicals and fertilizers. Similarly, a fusing system can be made of batteries, cell-phone or chemical reactions. In short, an IED is a collection of items that are not designed, produced or intended to be together [Thurman 2006].

3.2. Primary Effects of IEDs

IEDs follow similar patterns of destruction and damage to people. We can divide these effects into several sub-groups such as blast effect, fragmentation, projectiles, claymore and platter charge. Although, there will be collateral damage as well like building collapse etc., these effects can help us determine the intention of the person who engineered the bomb, and by following the same bombing signatures one can determine whether multiple bombings have used the explosives developed by the same person or organization [Thurman 2006]. An IED can also use an incendiary material to have a greater fireball or incendiary effect on the target.

Table 3.1 gives an approximate relationship between dynamic pressures and wind velocities calculated for sea level conditions [White 1959]. The data was obtained by manual digitization from the curves presented in the respective references [Rawlins 1977].

Table 3.1. Peak overpressure and corresponding wind velocities
[Adapted from White 1959, Rawlins 1977]

Overpressure PSI	Wind Velocity (mph)
0.02	40
0.1	70
0.6	160
2.0	290
8.0	470
16.0	670
40.0	940
125.0	1500

3.3. TNT Equivalence of Explosive Materials

With so many different explosives available, it would be extremely useful
to be able to compare all explosive materials on an equal footing. Bashera
[Beshara 1994] states that most of the data related to explosions used TNT,
and thus data related to any other explosive should be benchmarked against
its TNT equivalent. This can be done by relating some measure of the
explosive energy produced with x amount of an explosive to that produced
by an equivalent amount of TNT. However, the equivalence may be
affected by material shape (e.g., flat, square), number and type of explosives,
confinement, nature of source and pressure range being considered [Baker
1973]. So the comparison is only an approximation, the energy output W_{TNT}
for explosive material relative to that of TNT can be expressed as:

$$W_{TNT} = \frac{H_{exp}}{H_{TNT}} w_{exp} \qquad \text{Eq. 3.1}$$

where W_{TNT} is the equivalent TNT charge weight, H_{TNT} is the heat of
detonation of TNT, H_{exp} is the heat of detonation of the explosive, and
w_{exp} is the explosive weight. Table 3.2 gives the TNT equivalents (W_{TNT}) of
commonly used explosives in civilian and military applications:

Table 3.2. Explosives and their TNT equivalences [Krauthammer 2008]

TNT Factor	Explosive	TNT Factor	Explosive
1.1	*Amatol 80/20*	1	*TNT*
1.1	*M1 Dynamite*	1.1	*C4*
1.2	*Tetrytol 75/25*	0.4	*Ammonium nitrate*
1.2	*Tetryl*	0.8	*Ammonium nitrate with fuel oil*
1.1	*Sheet Explosives M118/M186*	0.1	*Natural gas*
1.5	*NitroGlycerin*	0.9	*Ammonium Picrate*
1.1	*Bangalore Tarpedo (M1A2)*	1.0	*HBX-3*
1.1	*Shaped Charges (M2A3, M2A4, M3A1)*	1.0	*Military Dynamite (MVD)*
1.3	*Composition B*	1.1	*Pentolite*
1.3	*Composition C4 and M112*	1.2	*Torpex*
1.6	*PETN*	0.9	*Tritonal*
1.6	*RDX*	0.5	*Black Powder*

3.4. Basic Scaling Laws

The amount of explosive energy released and the nature of the propagation medium determine the characteristics of the blast wave generated by an explosion. Experiments have been carried out to measure these properties under control conditions with a given reference set of explosion data. The experimental results can be used to obtain data for other explosions using scaling laws. Readers are directed to [Baker 1983, Baker 1973] for a comprehensive description of explosive scaling laws and their properties.

The cube root scaling law is the most commonly used form of blast scaling. This law states that when two charges of the same explosive and geometry (but of different size) are detonated in the same atmosphere, the shock waves produced are similar in nature at the same scaled distances. Two explosions can be expected to give identical blast wave peak overpressures at distances which are proportional to the cube root of the respective energy release. For example, to produce a given blast overpressure at twice a given distance requires eight times the explosive energy release, e.g., a person 20 feet away from a blast receives 9 times less blast force than somebody who is 10 feet from the explosion [Crabtree 2006]. The scaled distance or the proximity factor Z, is defined as [Cooper 1996]:

$$Z = \frac{R}{(WT_a/P_a)^{1/3}} \qquad \text{Eq. 3.2}$$

where R is the distance from the center of the explosion to the target location in feet, W is the energy release, or amount of TNT in kilograms, in the explosion to be described, T_a is the ambient temperature in Kelvin, and P_a is the ambient pressure in bars. Using this scaling law one can determine the blast overpressure on any given point from the explosion to the target.

3.5. Explosive Models

In order to model the effects of a suicide bomber on a given crowd formation, it is essential to properly model the deleterious properties of the blast waves. A simulation which seeks to study the impact of a suicide bomber on casualty rates and injuries related to crowd formation must be able to adequately model the influence of peak overpressure, duration and impulse of the explosion. The next few sections discuss the injury models we have used in our simulation.

To plug-in any of the following explosive models, scaling laws for explosions based on geometrical similarity are used. By using the scaling law, the distance at which a given peak overpressure is produced by a reference explosion may be scaled up or down to provide a corresponding distance for other explosions. All simulations considered in this study use either the one pound TNT curve, as show in respective models, or a given equation. Different explosives can also be considered, however, by modifying the overpressure versus distance history or by utilizing data specific to the explosive compositio Eq. 3.1n.

The time duration of a blast wave must also be considered because the magnitude of injury depends in part on how long the damaging forces are applied. Because of the relationship between the speed associated with the initial shock front and the changing local speed of sound as the blast wave propagates, the duration of the blast wave increases with distance from the center of the explosion, and reaches a limiting maximum value (and also vanishes) as the shock front degenerates into a sound wave. To model duration increase as a function of distance from the origin of the explosion, a baseline set of data was used and a scaling law employed. Blast wave duration at the bomber's location can be varied from 0.5 milliseconds to 2.0 milliseconds, and the duration will increase in proportion to the scaled data set. In other words following the same shape, but corrected for time and distance [Gilbert and Kenneth 1985].

Impulse is also an important aspect of the damage-causing ability of the blast, and may become a controlling factor for short duration, small yield explosives. The significant portion of the impulse is associated with the positive phase. The decay of blast overpressure does not follow a typical logarithmic decay relation, because the overpressure drops to zero in finite time. A quasi-exponential form for pressure, in terms of a decay parameter α, and of a time t, which is measured from the instant the shock front arrives can be given as [Gilbert and Kenneth 1985]:

$$p = p_0 \left[1 - \frac{t}{t_d}\right] e^{\frac{-\alpha t}{t_d}} \qquad \text{Eq. 3.3}$$

where p is the instantaneous overpressure at time t, p_0 the maximum or peak overpressure observed when t is zero, and, t_d, the time duration. The decay parameter is also a measure of intensity of the shock system. Equation (2) may also be used in the simulation if the decay parameter α is specified. For example to determine the evolution of the positive phase duration as a function of distance from the explosive center.

Table 3.3 presents an overview of the explosive models presented in the next sections with input distances, overpressure output, datasets and their respective references.

Table 3.3. Comparison of Explosive Models Input and Output

S#	Models	Distance	Overpressure	Duration (Td)	Dataset	Ref
1	Paul Cooper	Scaled Distance [Z = R/Wta/Pa)^1/3]	Po/Pa	Scaled Duration (ms)	Discretized	[Cooper 1996]
2	Harold Brode	Radial Distance (ft)	P/Px	Actual Duration (ms)	Tabular	[Brode 1957]
3	Kingrey-Bulmsah	Scaled Distance [Z = R/ft/lb^1/3]	Incident Overpressure PSI		Discretized	[Bogosian, Ferritto, and Shi 2002]
4	J. Clutter with Reflection	Scaled Distance X/R	Incident Overpressure PSI		Discretized	[Clutter, Mathis, and Stahl 2006]
5	Henrych Smith	Scaled Distance [Z = R/m/kg^1/3]	Kpa		Equation	[Shrapnack, Jhonson, and Phillips 1991]
6	U.S. Army	Scaled Distance [Z = R/ft/lb^1/3]	Incident Overpressure PSI		Equation	[Mayo and Kluger 2006]
7	Kinney-Gilbert	Scaled Distance [Z = R/m/kg^1/3]	N/M2		Equation	[Gilbert and Kenneth 1985]

3.5.1. Paul Cooper Model

Experimental and theoretical means have been used to obtain important parameters associated with blast waves. A theoretical analysis for peak overpressure utilizes the same mathematical approach as for a planar shock wave, but includes the effects of spherical divergence and the transient nature of the blast event [Cooper 1996, Gilbert and Kenneth 1985]. As an example, values for the peak overpressure generated in a standard atmosphere for the blast wave generated from a one-pound spherical charge of TNT are shown in Figure 3.3.

For the wave at distances far from the center of the explosion, the blast wave behaves as a sound wave, and its energy-distance relation follows an inverse square law. The intensity of sound energy is proportional to the square of sound pressure, so that a simple inverse relation between peak overpressure and distances sufficiently great ensures that the blast wave overpressure approaches zero. Also shown in Figure 3.4 is the peak overpressure that would be expected at various distances had the energy released by the one-pound point source of TNT been concentrated into a point source. It can be seen by comparing the two curves that the effect of the finite size of explosive charge source is initially to spread out the energy and reduce the peak overpressure, and that this effect holds out to some appreciable distance from the center of the explosion – around 5 charge diameters. At intermediate distances, the large amounts of gas produced from the TNT begin to become evident in the peak overpressure curve. At greater distances losses due to dissociation and ionization become evident in the point source and act to reduce the energy available from a point source so that peak overpressure observed far from a point source are somewhat less than those from TNT with the same energy release. This demonstrates that although knowing the total energy release is important, it is inadequate to completely describe the blast event. In our simulations, either the point source or spherical TNT charge can be selected, with the TNT charge giving more realistic, and higher, estimates of casualty and injury rates.

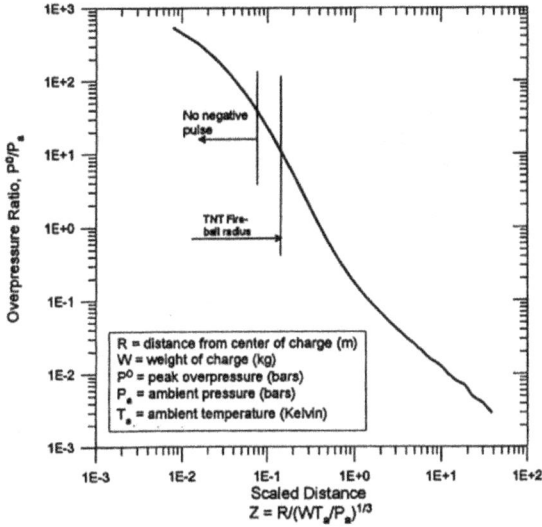

Figure 3.3. Peak overpressure ratio versus distance for explosions with a yield of one pound of TNT [Cooper 1996].

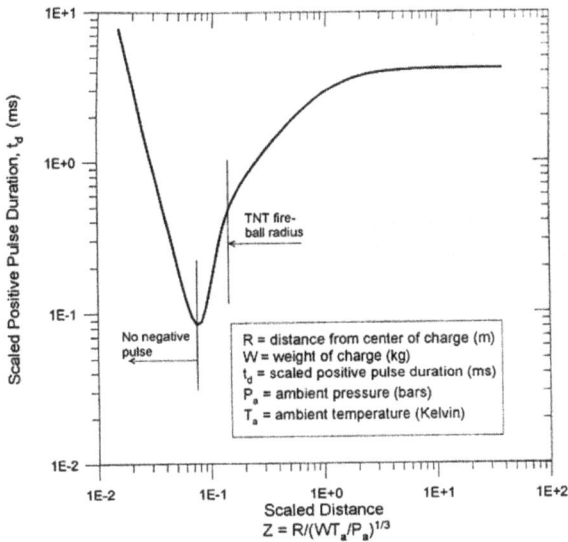

Figure 3.4. Scaled positive pulse duration Vs. Scaled Distance [Cooper 1996].

3.5.2. Harold Brode Model

This model, for the prediction of incident peak overpressure ratio, was originally created by Harold Brode in 1957 [Brode 1957], and later popularized by Kinney and Gilbert through their work "Explosives Shocks in Air", [Gilbert and Kenneth 1985]. Figure 3.5 shows the curve for this model; values of the peak overpressure are generated in normal ambient pressure using one pound of spherical TNT charge.

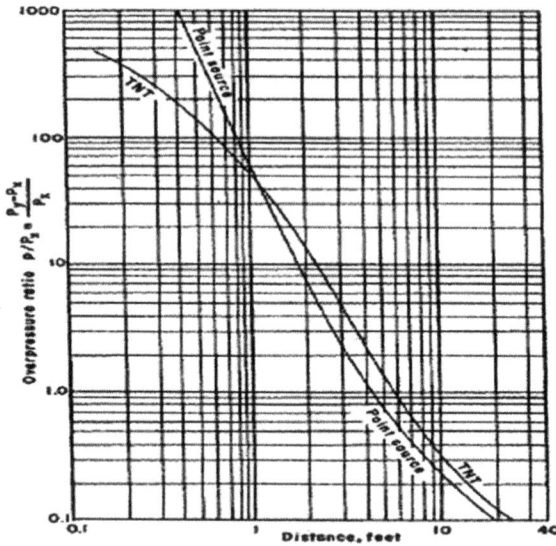

Figure 3.5. Peak overpressure ratio versus distance for explosions with a yield of one pound of TNT [Adapted from Brode 1957].

3.5.3. Kingrey-Bulmash Model

The Kingrey-Bulmash model is the widely used for the prediction of incident peak overpressure. A good number of software and army devices use this model, like ConWep and BlastX. It has been also reported in US army reports such as TM 5-1300 [Bogosian, Ferritto, and Shi 2002].

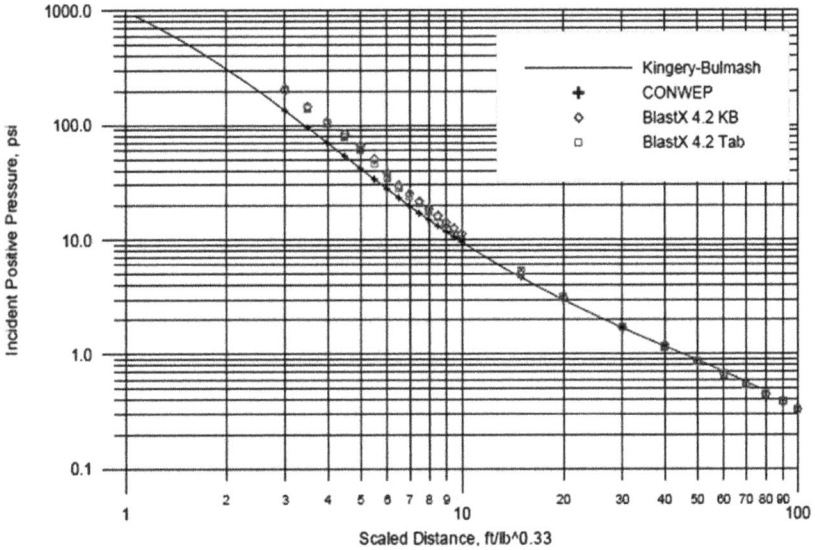

Figure 3.6. Kingrey-Bulmash Model [Adapted from Bogosian, Ferritto, and Shi 2002]

3.5.4. J. Clutter with Reflection

Clutter *et al.* realized the need for a separate model in the case of reflection when a person is standing next to the reflecting surface, and thus would be the victim of high overpressure. This model has been used for the estimation of reflection waves from rigid surfaces [Clutter, Mathis, and Stahl 2006 2006].

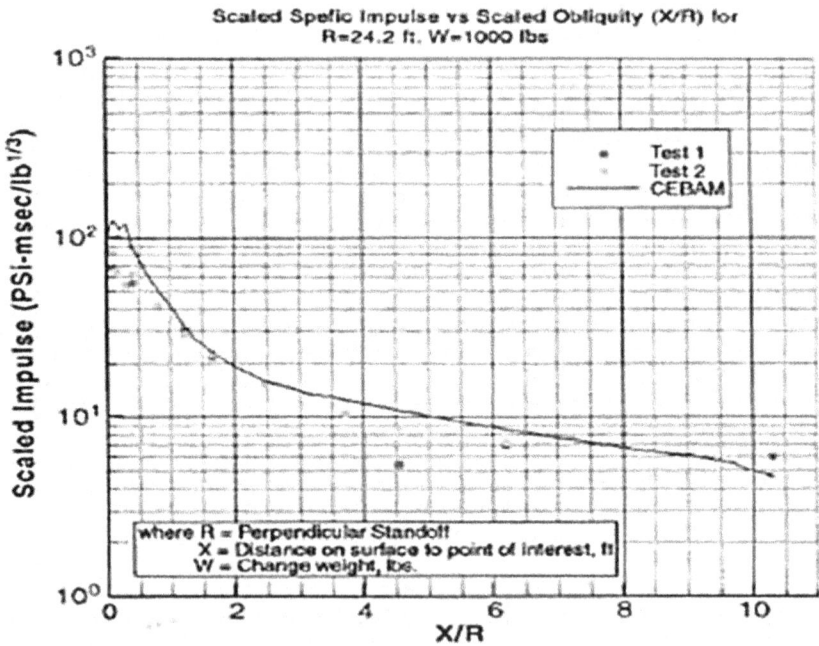

Figure 3.7: Peak overpressure Vs Scaled Distance
[Clutter, Mathis, and Stahl 2006 2006]

3.5.5. Henrych Smith Model

Explosive models tend to favor far-field effects over near-field overpressure, and continuously underestimate the pressure at distances very close to the point of explosion. To overcome this problem Henrych Smith [Shrapnack, Jhonson, and Phillips 1991] gives the following set of equations to better predict the overpressure ratio.

$$P = \frac{1407.2}{Z} + \frac{554.0}{Z^2} + \frac{35.7}{Z^3} + \frac{0.625}{Z^4} \quad 0 \le Z \le 0.3$$

$$P = \frac{619.4}{Z} + \frac{32.6}{Z^2} + \frac{213.2}{Z^3} \quad 0.3 < Z \le 1.0$$

$$P = \frac{66.2}{Z} + \frac{405.0}{Z^2} + \frac{328.5}{Z^3} \quad 1.0 < Z \le \infty$$

where Z is the scale distance.

3.5.6. US Army Model

The U.S. Army uses the following equation to estimate the incident peak overpressure at a given distance from the point of explosion [Mayo and Kluger 2006].

$$P_o = \frac{4120}{Z^3} - \frac{105}{Z^2} + \frac{39.5}{Z}$$

where, again, Z is the scale distance.

3.5.7. Kinney Gilbert Model

Based on Harold Brode's experiments and tabular data, Kinney and Gilbert developed the following equation [Gilbert and Kenneth 1985] which is now widely accepted and used in blast loading literature and research.

$$\frac{P}{P_a} = 101325 \frac{808.0\left(1+\frac{z}{4.5}\right)^2}{\sqrt{1+\left(\frac{z}{0.048}\right)^2}\sqrt{1+\left(\frac{z}{0.32}\right)^2}\sqrt{1+\left(\frac{z}{4.35}\right)^2}}$$

Where,

P = Overpressure value

Pa = Atmospheric Pressure, (Sea level value of 101,325

3.6. Blast Forensics

It is very important for blast loading analysis, and any simulation that deals with the precise prediction of explosive incident peak overpressure, that we have the right and accurate input. A smaller change in input variables or strength of the explosive can lead to significantly different results. The following section presents the basic methods in the measurement of explosive characteristics from a blast scene.

3.6.1. Swabbing

The systematic collection of organic and inorganic residues of explosives from a blast scene is called *Swabbing*. There are dozens of porous and nonporous items as witnesses of the blast at the scene. A trained professional can collect items like metals, glass, painted wood, stone, concrete, seat cushions, and fabric for explosive residues, and later send them to a laboratory for further testing and analysis. An important issue in swabbing is that the person doing the swabbing should wear commercial swabbing gear, so as to not contaminate the scene [Thurman 2006, Lenz 1976]. To better document and search a blast area, examiners often divide the area into different grid zones/cells.

3.6.2. Overpressure as Damage Markers

Using the scaling law described in Section 3.3, it is easy to calculate the pressure at other locations when pressure at one location is known using the following equation [Noon 2000].

$$P_1 = C, a \; know \; amount \; at \; distance \; r1$$

$$P_2 = P_1 \left[(r_1)^3 \Big/ (r_2)^3 \right] \qquad \text{Eq. 3.4}$$

Where *r1* is the distance of first location from the source of explosion, *r2* is the distance of second location from the source of explosion, and *P1* is the overpressure PSI received at the first location.

Damage markers often help in blast forensics to determine the blast overpressure at certain locations, and to find out the total strength of the explosive being used. For example, it is known that a glass window breaks at 0.5 to 1.0 psig (PSI gauge), therefore by using the broken window at the farthest distance from the point of explosion, a pathway of the explosion front or overpressure profile can be produced. Similarly, we can use the same method for other items whose weights can be estimated and that have been lifted, moved or thrown out due to the explosion (such as cars, plants etc.)

First-cut estimate of an amount of explosive yield can also be measured by the scatter of debris, using the following equation:

$$W = [r^3]/K \qquad \text{Eq. 3.5}$$

where r = the distance of farthest scatter debris from the point of explosion, W = amount of explosive yield (Kg of TNT), and K = scaling factor, 91,000 m3/kg.

4. How to Model Blast Injuries in a Suicide Bombing Attack

"Sometimes a scream is better than a thesis."

~ Ralph Waldo Emerson

Blast injury is the physiological insult to the human organs due to an explosion [Ciraulo 2006]. The exact explosive mass used in suicide attacks is hard to determine. However, it is possible to give some general indications of the overall level of injuries to be expected based on the size of an explosion, the number of participants and crowd formation. To predict the blast injuries with accuracy, one has to predict the time history of the blast wave in the air for static and dynamic overpressure, duration of the force being exerted on the person or object as a result of the explosion and the response of the person or structure to that loading [ICE 1994]. For a fast and easy estimate with sufficient accuracy, overpressure alone is the key predictor when compared against the tabulated data or available injury models in the literature. Human injury is usually caused by direct blast wave overpressure, secondary effects like fragmentation and shrapnel, or the whole body translation. There are other reasons as well, like toxic inhalation, ground shock and thermal radiation, but these are considered to be insignificant when compared with overpressure and missile impact injuries [Davies 1993].

There are two types of loading effects that are responsible for almost all injuries in humans: diffraction loading and drag. Diffraction loading is dependent on the peak overpressure (that is the pressure above ambient pressure, often called side-on pressure). It is the force exerted on a human or object during the blast wave envelopment process upon and around the exposed victim/object (i.e., Stress waves) [Singer, Cohen, and Stein 2005, Davies 1993]. This loading applies the crushing forces on the object/ human that come due to the pressure differential in internal and external environment. Drag loading is usually caused by the transient winds that come along with the passage of the blast wave (i.e., Shear waves) [Davies 1993, Abbasi and Khan 1998, Singer, Cohen, and Stein 2005]. It depends on dynamic pressure of a shock wave.

The amount of explosive charge, distance from the point of explosion and the surrounding environment (Open, Confined, Water) determine the peak overpressure [Linsky and Miller 2006]. The strength of the peak overpressure and the duration of the blast wave is directly proportional to the amount of explosive being used. The duration is usually between 2 to 10 milliseconds for typical suicide bombing attacks. A suicide bomber usually carries 10 to 30 pounds of TNT equivalent, while a car can carry up to 500 pounds or more [Linsky and Miller 2006].

All things being equal, if the impact of projectiles is ignored, a person oriented with the long axis of their body perpendicular to the reflecting surface will have higher chances of injury and death, compared to ones who are not nearby a reflecting surface, or who lie parallel to the blast wind [Dire 2007]. A blast wave is highly destructive because of its rapid external loading, and organs that are slower to equilibrate with external stress are more susceptible for harm, like all air-containing organs (Lungs, Kidney, Bowels etc).

4.1. Types of Blast Injuries

Injuries that occur as a result of explosions can be grouped into several broad categories, as primary, secondary, tertiary and miscellaneous injuries. Primary injuries are caused by the direct result of pressure wave impacting and travelling through the body. This includes rupture of tympanic membranes, pulmonary damage, rupture of hollow viscera etc. Secondary injuries result from flying debris, projectiles and shrapnel that damage the body. This includes penetrating trauma and fragmentation injuries. Tertiary blast injuries result from the victim's body being thrown by the blast wind, and then impacting stationary objects, whole body displacement and subsequent de-acceleration impact against a rigid object [Mohanty 1998]. This includes crushing injuries and blunt trauma, penetrating trauma, fractures and traumatic amputations. Miscellaneous blast injuries are caused by flame and chemicals that include burns, asphyxia and exposure to toxic inhalants.

There are three kinds of tissue damage mechanisms during an explosion: Spalling, Implosion, and Inertia. In spalling, the blast wave causes vibration, tears in tissue walls, hemorrhage, and the loss of structural integrity when it passes from high density areas to low density areas of air-filled organs, like lungs, intestinal lumen, middle ear, bowels etc [Briggs 2003]. Implosion cause serious damage and rupture of solid organs, and the areas of attachment due to extreme compression and expansion of organs when the blast wave exits. In addition, inertia causes damage with the moving ability of acceleration and de-acceleration of people and stationary objects [Foltin 2006].

4.1.1. Primary Blast Injuries (PBI)

Primary blast injuries are caused by the deleterious effects of the blast wave passing through the body (usually called barotraumas – overpressure or under-pressure [DePalma, Burris, and Champion 2005]). The magnitude of this wave depends on the type, size and medium of explosion [Briggs 2003]. The higher-frequency stress and lower-frequency sheer waves of the explosion have little or no effect on solid or fluid-filled organs (because they are less compressible). Their primary target is air-filled organs such as lungs, kidneys, gestational intestine tract and hallows viscera. The blast wave causes an extreme pressure differential in these organs to disrupt and destroy the tissues [Ciraulo, David, and Frykberg 2006]. A low-level shear can compromise the integrity of vascular beds and cause hemorrhage, while a high-level shear can lead to serious mechanical failures [Dire 2007]. The effects of these waves increase in close and confined spaces [Briggs 2003]. An overpressure of as low as 5 psi can rupture tympanic membrane, 16 psi can cause blast lung injury, and 30 to 42 psi is considered the lethal threshold limits [Dire 2007]. PBI cause more local disruption and disintegration of directly exposed tissues [Ferris 1998]. Table 4.1 shows categories of PBI.

Table 4.1. Categories of PBI [Adapted from Sharpnack, 1991]

System	Injury
Respiratory	pulmonary hemorrhage, alveolovenous fistula (air-embolism production), airway epithelial damage
Circulation	cardiac contusion, myocardial ischemic change
Digestive	gastrointestinal hemorrhage, gastrointestinal perforation, retroperitoneal hemorrhage, ruptured spleen or liver
Eye and Orbit	retinal air embolism, orbital fracture
Auditory	tympanic membrane rupture, ossicular fractures, cochlear damage

4.1.2. Secondary Blast Injuries (SBI)

SBI refers to injuries caused by flying debris, metal projectiles, blast fragments, shredded glass and shrapnel [Briggs 2003]. Fragments are usually the disintegrated pieces of explosion carrier (pipe, suit case etc.), while shrapnel (named after Henry Shrapnel – Developer of anti-personnel military munitions) are added metal pieces (like screws, bolts, nuts) that cause penetrating wounds and damage. Injuries caused by penetrating wounds are the leading cause of death in a typical suicide bombing attack [Mayo and Kluger 2006, [DePalma, Burris, and Champion 2005]. The intensity of wounds depends on the size, shape, velocity, and the type of fragments. Victims can also have significant protection from SBI by protective gear, clothing and other individuals and objects in the vicinity (who act as a shield). SBI usually occurs in exposed areas such as the head, neck, and limbs [DePalma, Burris, and Champion 2005]. Common examples of SBI include traumatic amputations, fractures, bruising, abrasion, laceration and soft tissue injuries [Ferris 1998].

4.1.3. Tertiary Blast Injuries (TBI)

There are basically two kinds of TBI. One is caused by propulsion of the body into solid objects, and the second is caused by structural collapse of buildings, walls and ceilings due to blast overpressure [Briggs 2003,

Ferris 1998]. The dynamic pressure from the blast wind can also cause limb amputation, although it is not common [Mayo and Kluger 2006]. Common examples of TBI include head, spine, extremity and crush injuries [Briggs 2003, DePalma, Burris, and Champion 2005].

4.1.4. Miscellaneous Blast Injuries (MBI)

All other injuries directly or indirectly related to the blast can be grouped together in miscellaneous blast injuries (MBI). This includes toxic inhalation, thermal and radiation burns, additional injuries due to structural collapse and delay in transportation due to debris [Briggs 2003].

4.1.5. Percentage of Injuries and Triage

Table 4.2 presents the categories, mechanism and percentage of blast injuries. A point to remember here is that blast injuries do not occur in isolation, so a person with blast lung will most probably also have penetrating glass shreds, traumatic amputation, burns, inhalation injury and deafness. Table 4.3 shows an interesting analysis of the percentage of penetrating wounds in a few famous clashes, and Table 4.4 presents a patients' triage map for events like suicide bombing.

Table 4.2. Categories, mechanism, and percentage of blast injuries [Mahoney 2009, Ferris 1998, Marti 2006, Moore 2006, Stein and Hirsberg 1999, NATO 2003].

Category	Mechanism of Injury	Type of Injury	Primary target organs	%
Primary	Blast Wave Results from the impact of the over-pressurization wave with body surfaces.	Complete tissue disruption; partial tissue disruption; internal organ damage. Blast lung, TM rupture, middle ear damage, abdominal hemorrhage and perforation, Globe (eye) rupture, Concussion (TBI without physical signs of head injury). Bowel perforation and hemorrhage, mesenteric shear injuries, solid organ lacerations, eye perforation, ossicular disruption, cochlear damage.	Ears, lungs, gastrointestinal tract, central nervous system. Gas-filled structures are most susceptible (lungs, GI tract, and Middle Ear).	24

Secondary	Victim struck by flying debris. Results from flying debris and bomb fragments.	Injuries and stippling from explosive device; impact from flying debris. Penetrating ballistic (fragmentation) or blunt injuries, eye penetration (can be occult).	Skin, central nervous system, eye, musculoskeletal system. Any body part may be affected.	43
Tertiary	Victim impacted against stationary object; injuries by collapsing buildings. Results from individuals being thrown by the blast wind	Crush injuries, acceleration and deceleration impact injuries, vagal inhibition. Fracture and Traumatic amputation, close and open brain injury	Head injuries; skin; musculoskeletal system. Any body part may be affected.	19
Miscellaneous	Inhalation of dust or toxic gases, radiation etc. All explosion related injuries, illness, or disease not due to primary, secondary, or tertiary mechanism, includes exacerbation or complications of existing conditions, Toxic and dust inhalation, gases, radiations, crush injuries caused by falling debris, flash burns etc.	Burns, respiratory failure, etc. Burns (flash, partial and full thickness). Crush injuries, close and open brain injuries, asthma, COPD or other breathing problems from dust, smoke or toxic fumes, angina, hyperglycemia, hypertension.	Skin; eye; respiratory system Any body part may be affected	14

Table 4.3. Anatomical distribution of penetrating wounds as a percent [Adapted from Mahoney 2009].

Conflict	Head and Neck	Thorax	Abdomen	Limbs
World War I	17	4	2	70
World War II	4	8	4	75
Korea	17	7	7	67
Vietnam	14	7	5	74
Northern Ireland	20	15	15	50
Israel 1975	13	5	7	40
Israel 1982	14	4	5	41
Falkland Island	16	15	10	59
Gulf War (UK)	6	12	11	71
Gulf War (US)	11	8	7	56
Afghanistan (US)	16	12	11	61
Chechnya (Russia)	24	9	4	63
Somolia	20	8	5	65
Average	15	9.5	7.4	64.6

Table 4.4. Triage of terrorism victims [Adapted from Moore 2006, NATO 2007, NATO 2003].

Priority	Triage Level	Physiological Description	Example of Injuries
4 (Low)	Dead	Life extinct, absent vital signs.	Injuries incompatible with life (decapitation, complete abruption), unconscious patients with nil spontaneous respiratory effort.
3	Walking Wounded	Patients who regardless of injuries are able to walk.	Lacerations, abrasions, contusions, upper body fractures. Injuries that might otherwise be considered significant.

SIMULATION of SUICIDE BOMBING

Priority	Triage Level	Physiological Description	Example of Injuries
2	2nd Priority	Injured patients who are unable to walk with a spontaneous respiratory effort of 10-29 breaths per minute and/or distal capillary refill <2 seconds.	Unconscious patients, leg fractures, mild to moderate respiratory distress.
1 (High)	Top Priority	Injured patients who are unable to walk with a spontaneous respiratory effort of <9 or >30 breaths per minute and/or distal capillary refill >2 seconds.	Unconscious patients, leg fractures, severe respiratory distress, patients with significant decreased perfusion.

4.2. Fragments and Shrapnel Injuries

Suicide bombers cannot rely on random objects that are present in the location of a bombing to generate a consistent pattern of secondary injuries. Therefore, it is common for them to include added metal fragments like nuts, bolts and screws to cause more damage [Crabtree 2006]. The fragments and shrapnel generated by an explosion can cause severe injuries to humans in the immediate vicinity and at large distance [Mohanty 1998, Abbasi and Khan 1998]. These airborne projectiles penetrate into the body and cause injuries from laceration to deep life-threatening wounds in the heart, liver or brain [Stein 2005]. The penetration of these fragments depends on the velocity, and fragment area to weight ratio. For smaller fragments (less than 15 g of size), 50% of skin penetration is 30 m/s (100 ft/s). For larger fragments (equal to or greater than 2 lb), 3 m/s (1o ft/s) velocity can cause serious damage [Mohanty 1998].

51

4.3. Confined and Open Injuries

The intensity and damage of injuries vary significantly in open and confined-space explosions. Confined spaces offer an amplified set of reflective waves to cause greater harm. Confined spaces have much higher mortality of 15.8% as compared to 2.8% in open space [Stein 2005]. According to another estimate, confined spaces can have 10% more fatalities compared to open spaces with the same amount and type of explosive [David 2008]. 33% of victims in open-space explosions are fatally or severely injured compared to 58% in confined spaces [David 2008].

4.4. Injury Models

Specifying the amount of TNT, using the scaling law of Section 3.4, and the overpressure versus distance curves of explosive models, or the estimation equations of Chapter 3, allows the calculation of the peak overpressure at any distance away from the explosive origin. Using this peak overpressure and the respective pulse duration, injury or fatality can be estimated using one of the injury models described in this section. The amount of explosive defines the overpressure limits and thus the medical consequences. There are numerous models available to map peak incident overpressure to human injuries. The models differ based on their empirical analysis and mode of data collection. Few models are based on peak overpressure measurements based on sensors, and then mapping those measurements to human injury. Similarly, few models are based on injury data gathered from living objects such as sheep, pigs, rats and dogs, and then scaled for humans. Then there are few models that report human injury due to blast peak overpressure without any information about how far the victims were from the blast origin. These models concluded their results based on total lung or body tissue disruption and the amount of overpressure required to have that disruption. Table 4.5 shows one such model, adapted from [Noon 2000].

Table 4.5. Blast Overpressure mapping to human injury [Noon 2000].

Pressure Level (psig)	Type of Damage or Injury
0.5-1.0	Breakage of glass windows
>1.0	Knock People down
1.0-2.0	Damage to corrugated panels or wood siding
2.0-3.0	Collapse of non reinforced cinder block walls
5.0-6.0	Push over of wooden telephone poles
>5.0	Rupture ear drum
> 15.0	Lung damage
> 35	Threshold for fatal injuries
> 50	About 50% fatality rate
> 65	About 99% fatality rate

According to the estimates by the Lovelace foundation, there is a 1% fatality chances at 20-35 PSI, 50% at 40-50 PSI, and 99% at 55-65 PSI [Lovelace 1959]. Another estimate with small variations indicates 1% fatality rate at 35 PSI, and 99% at 65 PSI [Ciraulo, David, and Frykberg 2006]. 80 PSI is approximately equals to 1500 mph wind velocity [Glasstone 1977]. There is general agreement that PSI of more than 200 is universally fatal [Stein and Hirsberg 1999], and eardrum ruptures at as low as 5 PSI [Mayo and Kluger 2006, Crabtree 2006, Stein 2005, Garth 1994]. 40 or less PSI generally does not harm human lungs, and 80 PSI can be considered lethal in more than 50% of the cases [Stein and Hirsberg 1999].

4.4.1. Catherine Lee Injury Model

As shown in Table 4.6, Catherine Lee reported that eardrum rupture can occur at 5 PSI, 15 PSI can damage human lungs, lethality threshold limits are at 30 to 42 PSI, there will be 50% fatality at 42-57 PSI, and one should expect 95-100% fatality at 58-80 PSI or more [Lee 2005].

Table 4.6. Catherine Lee Injury Model [Adapted from White 1959, Lee 2005].

Injury	Maximum PSI
Eardrum Rupture	5
Lung Damage	15
Lethality Threshold	30-42
Lethality 50%	42-57
Lethality 95-100%	58-80

4.4.2. C. T. Born Injury Model

Dr. C. T. Born reported and revised overpressure to human injury mappings of Mellor [Mellor and Cooper 1989, Born 2005]. According to their findings <150 KPa will produced minor injuries such as eardrum rupture, 150-350 KPa can cause moderate injuries including bruises and laceration, 350-550 KPa can lead to severe injuries with primary lung damage, while overpressure of more than 500 KPa can lead to life threatening injuries and death. Table 4.7 presents their findings.

Table 4.7. C. T. Born Injury Model [Adapted from Mellor 1989, Born 2005].

Injury	Overpressure (kPa)
Minor Injury	< 150
Moderate Injury	150-350
Severe Injury	350-550
Very Severe Injury or Death	>550

4.4.3. Charles Stewart Injury Model

Dr. Stewart revised and reported a model by Rice and Heck [Stewart 2006, Rice and Heck 2000] for the U.S. Army. This is the most conservative model in the literature with the least number of casualties. The model is consistent with other injuries. For example, according to this model 5 PSI can lead to eardrum rupture, 30-40 PSI for primary lung damage, and 100 PSI or more can lead to death. This model, however, reports 200 PSI for most likely death compare to other models that report most likely death around 80 to 100 PSI. Table 4.8 presents this model.

Table 4.8. Charles Stewart Injury Model [Adapted from Rice and Heck 2000].

Effect	Overpressure PSI
Frame House Destroyed	1-2
Typical commercial construction destroyed	3-5
Tympanic membrane rupture	5
Tympanic membrane rupture in 50% of patients	15
Possible lung injury	30-40
Reinforced concrete construction destroyed	40
Lung injury in 50% of patients	75
Possible Fatal Injuries	100
Death most likely	200

4.4.4. Bowen's Lethality Curves

Among all of the injury models, Bowen's lethality curves are the oldest, most widely accepted, and most widely used models for predicting human injuries based on blast overpressure. The Bowen's lethality curves were developed after a number of experiments on different kinds of animals including rats, dogs, sheep, monkeys, swine, goats, steers, hamsters, rabbits and pigs using numerous blasts with different pulse durations (0.24 to 400 milliseconds) and magnitudes. The results were then scaled for humans [Greer 2006]. Figure 4.1 presents the relative tolerance levels of similar injuries in humans and other mammals.

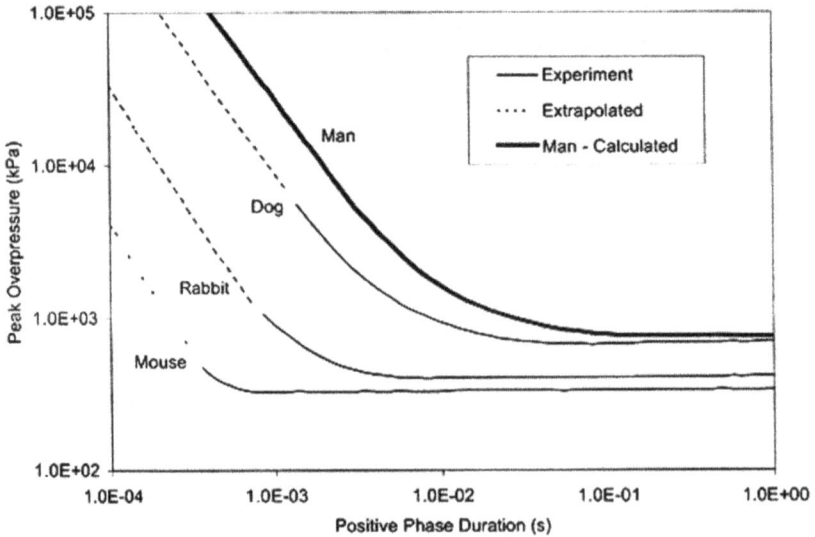

Figure 4.1. Relative tolerance level of humans and other mammals [Greer 2006]

The curves in Figure 4.1 can be used for free-field blast waves (Friedlander waves). [Greer 2006]. Using these Friedlander type curves, one can predict the impact from threshold lung injury to 99% probability of fatality [Greer 2006]. Original curves were scaled (and extrapolated) based on the mass and tolerance level of mammalian species for a 70-kg man [Cooper 1996, Greer 2006]. Figure 4.2, 4.3, and 4.4 show these curves for different situations. Figure 4.3 shows the fatality curves predicted for a 70-kg man, applicable to blast situations where the thorax is near a surface against which a shocked blast wave reflects at normal incidence, and where the long axis of the body is perpendicular to the direction of blast wave. The simplicity of these curves and the number of experiments performed to validate these findings makes them the first-choice to estimate the effects of blast loading on humans [Greer *et al.* 2005].

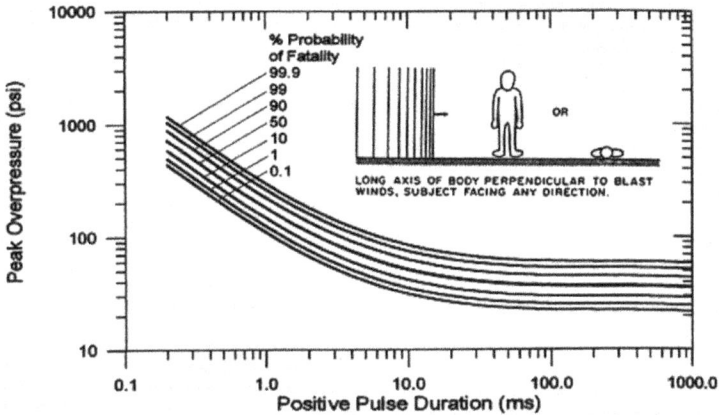

Figure 4.2. Fatality curves as a function of blast wave
peak overpressure and positive pulse duration
[Bowen, Fletcher, and Richmond 1968].

Figure 4.3 shows the fatality curves predicted for a 70-kg man applicable
to free-stream situations where the long axis of the body is parallel to the
direction of propagation of the blast wave, thus exposing the person only
to side-on pressure.

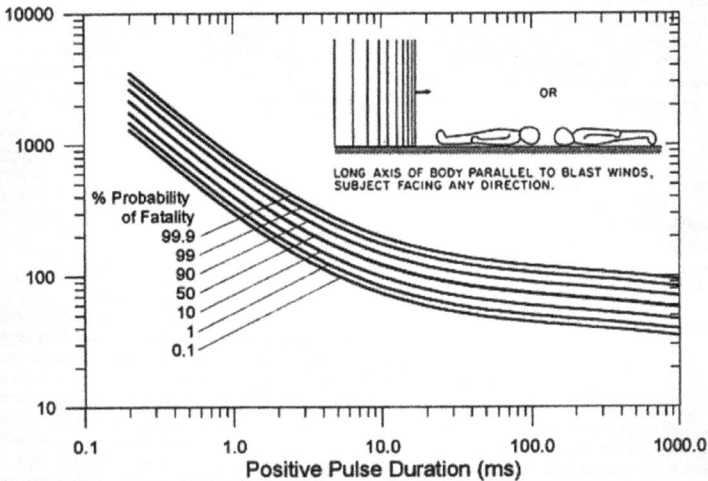

Figure 4.3. Fatality curves where the long axis of the body is parallel to
the direction of propagation of the shocked blast wave
[Bowen, Fletcher, and Richmond 1968].

Figure 4.4 shows the fatality curves predicted for a 70-kg man applicable to free-stream situations where the long axis of the body is perpendicular to the direction of propagation of the blast wave, and where the person is loaded with side-on pressure and dynamic pressure.

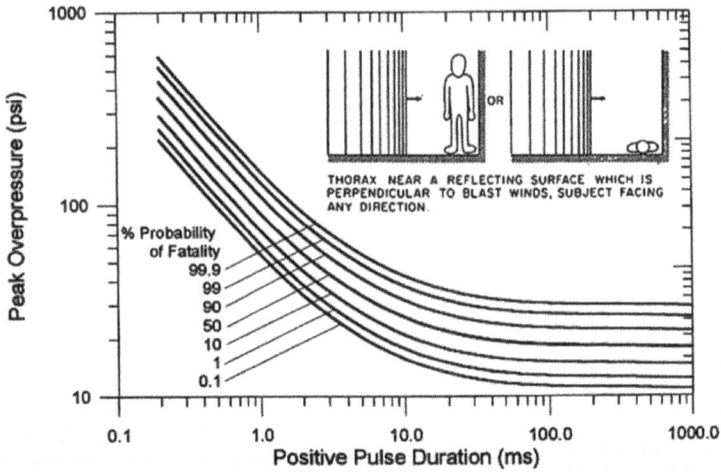

Figure 4.4. Fatality curves where the long axis of the body is perpendicular to the direction of propagation of the shocked blast wave [Bowen, Fletcher, and Richmond 1968].

4.4.5. Lethality Curves with Reflection

Figure 4.5 presents the Bowen's lethality curve with reflection model. The curves give the probability of a person near a reflecting surface (and thus loaded with reflected pressure) of being dead or injured based on pulse duration and peak overpressure PSI.

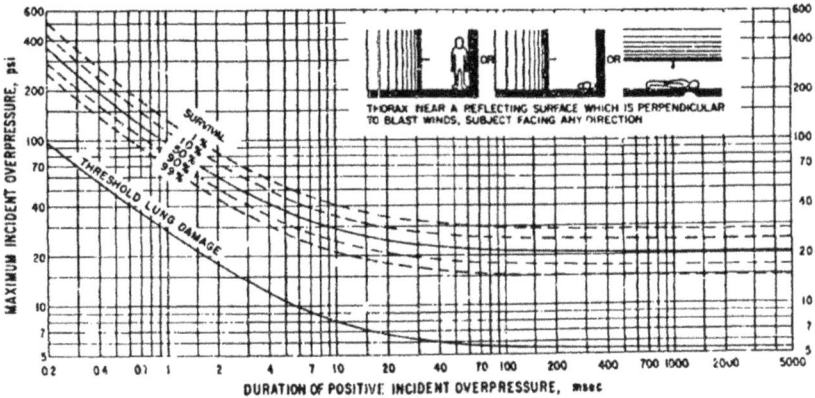

Figure 4.5. Lethality Curves for a 70-kg man who is near a reflecting surface [Bowen, Fletcher, and Richmond 1968].

4.4.6. ICE (Institute of Chemical Engineers) Injury Model

Humans are far less vulnerable to blast waves than buildings and structures. The disruption in the lungs is the number one cause of death in humans following a shock wave. The body response of a shock wave depends on amplitude and duration of the shock and body weight. A longer duration shock wave is more lethal than a short duration shock wave with the same level of impact [ICE 1994]. The Institute of Chemical Engineers has developed a following model for risk assessment in chemical industries and plants for accidental explosions and their effects on human beings. Figure 4.7 shows the probability of lung damage due to blast overpressure as a function of peak incident pressure Ps and incident impulse i with respect to body weight w. The model is based on extensive testing and experiments on animals and is fully applicable to human lung injuries [ICE 1994]. Figure 4.6 predicts that for an average weight man (160 pounds) a long duration shock of 70 PSI would lead to certain death, while the person requires almost 200 PSI for the same effect in case of a short duration shock wave. The same is true for lung damage where a long duration shockwave will require 10 PSI, compare to 30 PSI for a short duration shockwave for similar effects.

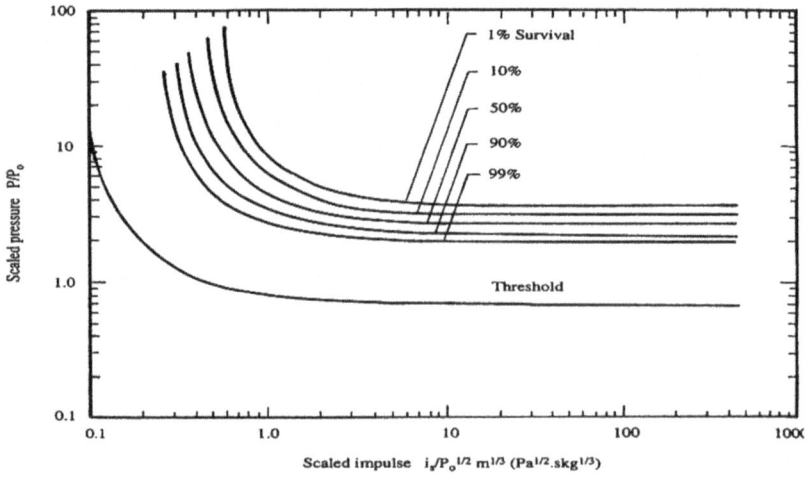

Figure 4.6. ICE Injury Model, *Ps* = ambient pressure, *Is* = impulse per square meter of the blast wave, *P* = overpressure, *m* = mass of target person [ICE 1994].

Following is an example to calculate the chances of survival for a 75-kg man, at atmospheric pressure Pa = 103 kPa (14.75 psi), subject to a blast overpressure Ps of 310 kPa (44.4 psig) and a duration t, of 10 ms, and Kg is the kilogram:

$$\text{Scaled overpressure } \bar{P}_s = \frac{P_s}{P_a} = \frac{310}{103} = 3.01$$

$$\text{Scaled Impulse } \bar{I}_s = \frac{I_s}{P_a^{0.5} \times m^{0.33}}$$

$$\text{Where } \bar{I}_s = (approx)\frac{P_s \times t}{2} = 310{,}000 \times 0.01 \times 0.5 = 1550 \, P_a s$$

$$\bar{I}_s = \frac{1550}{103{,}000^{0.5} \times 75^{0.33}} = 1.15$$

From the attached curve, we can see that this combination (of scaled overpressure = 3.01, vs. scaled Impulse = 1.15) gives a 90% chance of survival (10% lethal probability).

4.5. Safe Distance Approximations

According to David [David 2008], a general formula to measure the safe distance for a person from an explosive with fragmentation is as follows:

$$D = 600 \times \sqrt[3]{explosive\ weight\ in\ pounds} \qquad \text{Eq. 3.5}$$

Where D is the distance in feet.

For example, if the explosive weight is 10 pounds with fragmentation capability, the safe distance will be:

$$D = 600 \times \sqrt[3]{10}$$
$$D = 600 \times 2.1544 = 1292\ feet$$

Equation 4.2 gives a safe-distance formula for the explosive without fragmentation

$$D = 300 \times \sqrt[3]{explosive\ weight\ in\ pounds}$$

Table 4.9 shows an example safe-distance matrix. Similar table and matrices can be made for particular settings and industries to prevent death and injuries from accidental explosions. There are numerous estimation methods and tables available. One should take special consideration of the environment for when he/she wants to build the table. For example, does the environment have randomly placed objects that can act as projectiles in case of an accidental blast? Or is the plant in confined-space? For a rule of thumb, Stein [Stein 2005] suggests the distance of 16 meters to be safe from any serious injuries or death in case of a typical suicide bombing attack of 1-25 Kg of TNT.

Table 4.9. Safe-Distance Matrix [Adapted from David 2008].

Mechanism	Explosive Weight (TNT Equivalent) Kg	Lethal Range (Meters)	Severe Injury Range (Meters)
Suicide Bomber	1-5	5	10-30
Compact Car	227	30	450
Sedan	455	60	530
Passenger Van	1-180 (e.g., OKC)	80	840
Panel Truck	4,545 (e.g., Khobar)	91	1,150
Fuel Truck	13,636 (e.g., Beirut)	140	1,980
Semi-Trailer	27,273	180	2,130

5. Blockage and Fragmentation Modeling

This chapter provides an overview of crowd blockage, its effect on overall injury and lethality level, algorithms for two-dimensional and three-dimensional environments, statistical analysis of blockage, and the mechanism and details of fragmentation and projectiles.

5.1. Blockage

Blockage or shields present in a crowd can play an important role in the event of an explosion. Even a person providing a blockage in the line-of-sight between another person and an explosion can actually save that person's life by absorbing most of the shrapnel, or by consuming part of the blast wave overpressure. Spatial distribution of individuals in a crowd can therefore significantly alter the casualty toll, and different crowd formations can yield different outcomes with the same amount and type of explosive. This is true even when the average distance to the bomber between two different crowd configurations is identical.

This section introduces 2D and 3D models for finding the exact number of full and partial blockers between each person and the suicide bomber. Persons in the line of sight between a given target and the bomber are termed *full blockers*. Blockers who are not in the line of sight, but whose width covers some part of the body of the person from the blast projectiles, are referred as *partial blockers*. For example, imagine a person of 4 feet standing in front of a 6 foot person, or a person standing next to another. These persons, while not covering another person completely, can provide partial blockage. To the best of our knowledge, this study is the first to consider partial blockers in blast wave simulation.

5.1.1. Blockage in 2D

Each person is modeled in 2D by a line segment, where the mid-point of the line represents the position of the person, and the length represents their width. Each line in the model is represented by the coordinates of its two end points. The line between the mid-point of the target and the blast point is called the *line-of-sight*. Each target is also represented by a line called the *body-width-line*. The triangle, whose base is the body-width-line of the target and the blast point, is termed the *blast triangle*.

The line segment between the blast point (b_1, b_2) and the center of the target (t_1, t_2) is constructed and its slope is calculated. Assuming all people face towards the blast, the body-width-line of the target will be perpendicular to the line of sight. The slope of this line is the negation of the slope of the line of sight. Using simple coordinate geometry, one can easily determine the end points of the body-width-line of the target $((x,y):(z,w))$ given the mid-point of the line (t_1,t_2), the body width and the slope of the line. Given the end points of the body-width-line of the target, one can easily construct the two other sides of the blast triangle. The body-width-line of all other people in the scene are assumed to have the same slope as the slope of the body-width- line of the target. Taking this slope, the position coordinate, and the width, it is trivial to determine the end points of the body-width-line of each person.

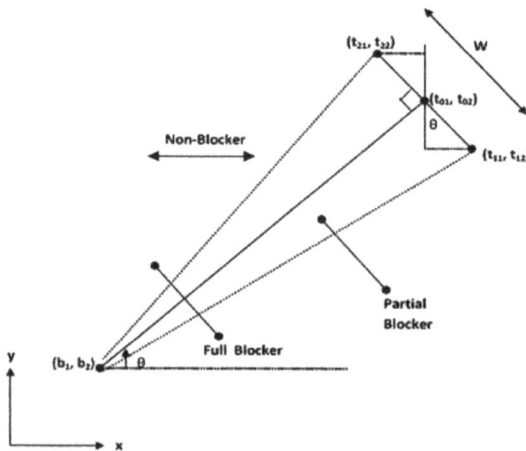

Figure 5.1. Full, partial and no blockers in 2D.

It is also worth noting that all infinite slopes are approximated by $\pm 1 \times 10^6$. In order to determine blockage, one has to determine if the body-width-line (representing a person) is intersecting with either the line-of-sight or the sides of the blast triangle. If a body-width-line is intersecting the line of sight, the person represented by this line is a full blocker. Otherwise, if it intersects with either side of the blast triangle, the person is a partial blocker. Figure 5.1 shows full and partial blockers in 2D.

5.1.2. Blockage in 3D

To find blockers in three-dimensions, a Cartesian(x-y-z) plane is used as a reference for the distribution of agents. Each agent (and non-living object) is modeled by a four-sided 2D polygon whose dimensions are determined by its height and width. The polygon is made to lie parallel to the y-z plane to reduce computational overhead. Figure 5.2 illustrate the concept.

There are four planes which enclose the cone whose vertex is the point of explosion and whose base is the four sided polygon modeling an agent. This cone is referred as the *blast cone* and the enclosing planes are referred as *blast cone planes*. The plane containing this polygon is called the agent body plane and the polygon is called the *agent body polygon*. The four line segments extending from the bomb position and the corner points of the polygon are called the *blast lines*.

An algorithm to identify blockage consecutively considers each agent as a target, and checks if any other agent is interfering with it from the blast point. A blocker is referred to as a *full blocker* if its four-sided polygon intersects the line of sight between the explosion and the target agent. An agent is referred to as a *partial* blocker if it is not a full blocker, and its four-sided polygon intrudes into the blast cone. To check if an agent is intruding into the blast cone, the smallest distance between the line of sight and the blast lines from the position point of the agent and the explosion is calculated. If this distance is less than half of the width of the agent, the line crosses the body plane between the polygon sides and the agent is considered a blocker. If the line is the line of sight, the agent is a full blocker, and if the line is only one of the blast lines, it is a partial blocker. If the smallest distance from each of the lines obtained is greater than half the width of the agents then it is not a blocker at all.

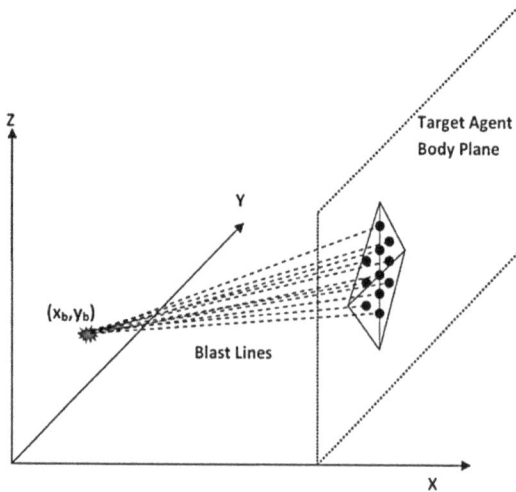

Figure 5.2. Blast cone originating from blast point in 3D.

To check if an agent is intruding into the blast cone, first we find the smallest distance between the line of sight and the blast lines from the position point of the agent and the bomb. If this distance is less than half of the width of the agent, the line apparently crosses the body plane between the polygon sides and the agent is considered a blocker. If the line is the line of sight, it will be full blocker and if the line is one of the blast lines, it will be considered a partial blocker. If the smallest distance from each of the lines obtained is greater than half of the width the agent it is not considered a blocker.

If an agent is a partial blocker, the percentage of blockage can also be determined by constructing additional lines that extend between the target agent body plane in the polygon area and the point of explosion. The percentage of lines crossing the body plane between the sides of the polygon is used as the percentage of partial blockage.

5.1.3. Statistical Analysis of Blockers

In this work we present a Monte Carlo simulation for simulating any given topology and event with blast and crowd characteristics. This section discusses the statistical analysis for the expectation of an agent being a blocker, and for determining how many agents and/or random simulation runs is required to obtain results with high levels of confidence.

To determine the probability of an agent being a blocker, if dropped randomly in the arena, can be calculated by the following method. The hypothetical situation is illustrated by Figure 5.3.

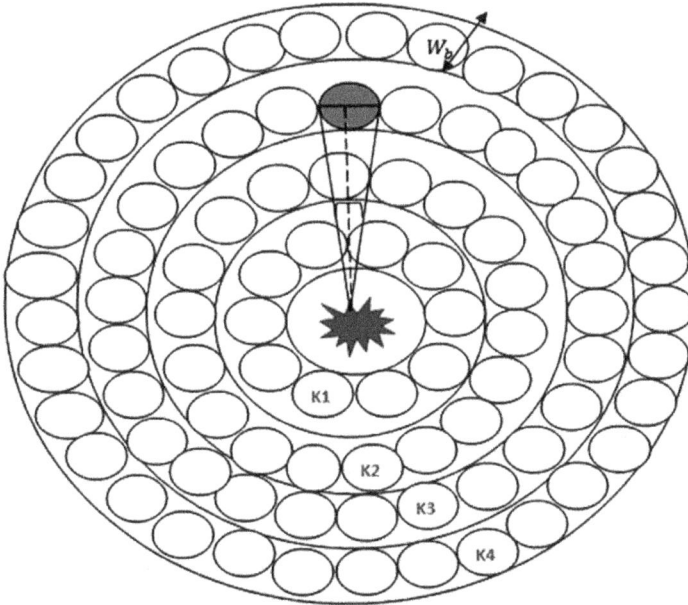

Figure 5.3: Agents in a situation with a bomber and blockers.

1. If W_b is an average width of an agent, and the radius of the arena is R, then the number of circles in the area is:

$$N_c = floor \left\lfloor \frac{R}{W_b} \right\rfloor$$

2. The maximum number of spots in the Kth circle is :

$$A_0 = (k-1)W_b + \frac{W_b}{2} = (k - \frac{1}{2})W_b$$

$$\theta_k = 2\tan^{-1}(\frac{W_b/2}{\left(K - \frac{1}{2}\right)W_b})$$

$$\theta_k = 2\tan^{-1}(\frac{1}{2K-1})$$

$$N_k = \frac{360°}{\theta_k}$$

3. The total number of Spots is :

$$N_s = \sum_{k=1}^{N_c} N_k$$

4. Probability of not being a blocker

   Assume that $N_A < N_S$ (Number of agents is less than number of Spots). The probability that an agent thrown into the arena is not a blocker is the probability that no spot behind it is occupied or partially occupied. Assuming uniform distribution of agents in the arena:

Probability of not being occupied a spot is given by:

$$P_{Not\ Occupied} = \frac{N_S - N_A}{N_S}$$

And, probability of not being a blocker is given by:

$$P_{Not\ Occupied} = \sum_{k=1}^{N_C} P_k \times (P_{Not\ Occupied})^{N_C - k}$$

Where P_k is the probability of being thrown into the kth circle is given by

$$P_k = \frac{N_K}{N_S}$$

Table 5.1 portrays the comparison of statistical results with actual simulation runs. The error margin of random Monte Carlo simulation result reduces with the number of runs and the number of agents. Therefore, if the user wants to run the simulation with only 5 agents, he/she should run it for at least 500 times to get the results with error margin of 0.003%, if the user has 250 or more agents, then 100 runs will be enough to yield results with the same confidence level.

Table 5.1. Comparison of expected statistical output with simulation runs.

	Agents	Stats	Simulation	Difference		Agents	Stats	Simulation	Difference
50 Runs	5	0.96	0.95	0.01	**100 Runs**	5	0.96	0.97	0.01
	10	0.89	0.84	0.05		10	0.89	0.86	0.03
	50	0.712	0.75	0.038		50	0.712	0.74	0.028
	100	0.536	0.55	0.014		100	0.536	0.52	0.016
	250	0.284	0.3	0.016		250	0.284	0.3	0.016
	500	0.155	0.15	0.005		500	0.155	0.154	0.001
Overall Error Margin				0.022166667	Overall Error Margin				0.016833333

	No of Agents	Stats	Simulation	Difference		No of Agents	Stats	Simulation	Difference
250 Runs	5	0.96	0.967	0.007	**500 Runs**	5	0.96	0.965	0.005
	10	0.89	0.87	0.02		10	0.89	0.885	0.005
	50	0.712	0.73	0.018		50	0.712	0.71	0.002
	100	0.536	0.53	0.006		100	0.536	0.53	0.006
	250	0.284	0.29	0.006		250	0.284	0.28	0.004
	500	0.155	0.154	0.001		500	0.155	0.155	0.000000
Overall Error Margin				0.009666667	Overall Error Margin				0.003666667

5.2. Fragmentation and Shrapnel

Improvised Explosive Devices (IEDs) typically use rigid containers like pipes, steel cases, or plastic bottles to enclose the explosive charge, which break into numerous pieces after an explosion. IEDs may also contain shrapnel such as nails, bolts, screws, and other pieces of metal around the main charge to produce higher casualties and damage. Pieces of the exploded container are usually called *fragments*, and the externally added metal such as nails and bolts are referred as *Shrapnel*.

The following sections explain the algorithm to simulate the effects of both kinds of projectiles for agents in an arena. IEDs may also contain a platter charge – a directional large piece of metal intended for a particular target like an armored vehicle. A platter charge is similar to blast fragments but with directional effect.

5.2.1. Fragments

The simulation has made the following assumptions:

1. Only the primary effect of a fragment is considered. This means a single fragment can make an impact to at most one agent.
2. The explosive case is assumed to be divided into 50 equally-sized mass fragments. This assumption can be changed based on the simulation environment or real-life scenario.
3. The trajectory of fragments is assumed to be a straight line and their speed is considered to be constant. Fragments are smaller in size and have very short flight time, thus the interference of gravitational forces is usually ignored.

The first step in simulating fragments is defining the fragments mathematically. Each fragment can be modeled by its initial position. A line passing through this initial position and the position of the bomber is the trajectory of the projectile. Hence, the trajectory of the ith fragment is modeled by $P_1:(x_i,y_i,z_i)$ – the initial position of the fragment and $P_2:(x_b,y_b,z_b)$ – the bomber position. The speed of each fragment at a given point is determined by the overpressure of the blast wave. Each fragment flies with this speed on the trajectory line until it encounters the body of an agent. The simulation determines whether a given fragment encounters the body of the agent using the following approach.

The impacted agents are the ones that may not be on the line of sight, but whose body width or size covers some part of the body of a person from the blast projectiles. The simulator calculates the shortest distance between the agent location and the trajectory line and checks if it is less than the body width of the agent. If the distance is less than the body width, then the fragment is going to have an impact on this particular agent. This is similar to the logic used to find partial blockers in the preceding section. A fragment is no longer considered in the simulation once it is found to have an impact on an agent. The simulation first sorts the agents according to the distance from the bomber in ascending order. Every agent is tested against every active fragment to find the fragments which impact which agent. The fragments that are found to have an impact on an agent will not be considered in the remaining part of the simulation and will be made inactive.

To determine the degree of impact a fragment has on an agent, the following two parameters are considered:

- What is the energy of the fragment before the impact?
- Which part of the body is impacted?

The theoretical initial speed of a fragment is given as follows:

$$v = 2 \cdot \Delta E \frac{m_c}{m_e} + K \frac{m_c}{m_e} \qquad \text{Eq. 5.1}$$

where ΔE is the heat of the explosive charge. For TNT, this value would be 2.175e6 J/kg. The quantities m_e and m_c are the masses of the explosive charge and the mass of the fragmentation casing. K is a geometrical constant and its values are given in the Table 5.2.

Table 5.2. Fragmentation device geometrical constants [Palmer 2005].

Shape	K
Flat Plate	1/3
Cylinder	1/2
Sphere	3/5

We can assume this velocity is constant. The energy before the impact is:

$$E = 12 m_p v_p^2 \qquad \text{Eq. 5.2}$$

where m_p is the mass of each fragments and v_p is the speed of each fragments obtained by Equation 5.1.

This issue needs some more steps on vector mathematics. First the plane containing an agent body will be defined. The next step will be determining the intersection point of the plane with the trajectory line of the fragment. Three points are sufficient to define a plane. We can take three non co-linear points to be:

P1:(x_1,y_1,z_1), **P2**:(x_2,y_2,z_2), and **P3**:(x_3,y_3,z_3)

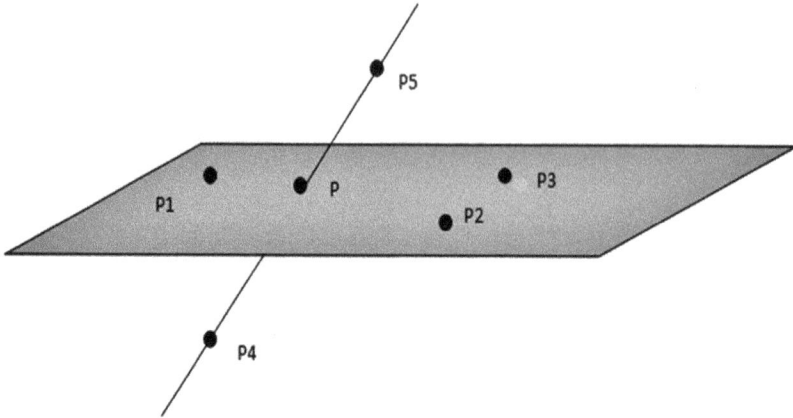

Figure 5.4. Intersection of the plane and line

In the simulation, these points are defined as **P1**:$(x_1,y_1,z_1) = (x_t, y_t, z_t)$, **P2**:$(x_2,y_2,z_2) = (x_t, y_t, z_t + h2)$, **P3**:$(x_3,y_3,z_3) = (x_t, y_t + w2, z_t)$, P4 and P5 are two distinct points in the trajectory line. These points in the simulation are defined as **P4**:$(x_4,y_4, z_4) = (x_b, y_b, z_b)$, **P5**: $(x_5,y_5, z_5) = (x_i, y_i, z_i)$.

The next step is to determine which part of the body this point represents. If $z \in (z_b, z_b+h2)$ and $y \in (y_b-w2, y_b+w2)$ then the impact will be considered to be in the chest or brain area. Otherwise, the impact will be considered as on the limbs. Note that the body plane is assumed to be parallel to the y-z plane in this simulation. An agent who encounters an impact around his chest by a high energy fragment will most probably die. Similarly, an agent whose limbs are impacted by a fragment whose energy is greater than the threshold energy will face serious injury. An agent whose limbs are impacted by a fragment whose energy is below the threshold energy or whose chest region is impacted by very low energy fragments will face minor injuries.

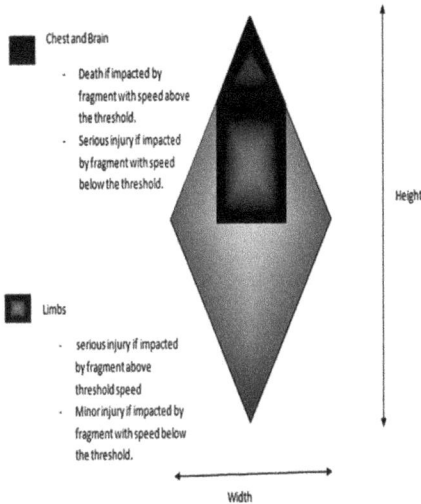

Figure 5.5. Impact on different parts of the body.

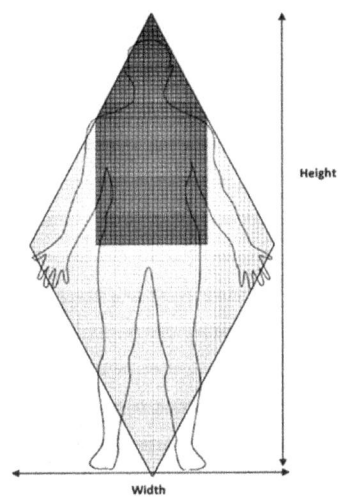

Figure 5.6. Target regions of the human body.

Figures 5.5 and 5.6 represent the exposed or target regions on the human body. Thus, knowing the speed of the fragments before an impact and which part of the body they impacted, we can determine the effect they bring on each agent. The cumulative effect of impacting fragments on an agent will determine the status of the agent after the blast.

5.2.2. Shrapnel and Claymore Effect

Shrapnel increases the lethality of an explosive device by higher injury to people and structural damages. Shrapnel are different from fragments – that are the parts of the explosive carrier or the body of the target. Shrapnel when used can easily be found in the epicenter of the blast and/or victims' bodies. On average a suicide bomber consumes 50% of the shrapnel being used in the explosive he/she is carrying [Kress 2004].

Shrapnel usually produce a *Claymore Effect* with an omni-directional spray of projectiles. Most IEDs are designed to burst in a flower bouquet pattern to throw the shrapnel horizontally between 2 and 6 feet above the ground. This pattern increases the chances of hitting a human's torso and head. To produce a claymore effect, the majority of shrapnel are placed on one side of the explosive to propel them towards a target for a greater damage.

Our simulation has incorporated a widely used shrapnel model developed by Moshe Kress at the Naval Postgraduate School in Monterey, California [Kress 2004]. Only the primary effect of the shrapnel is considered. This means single shrapnel can have an impact on at most one agent. The trajectory of the shrapnel is dependent on the initial dispersion angle. Shrapnel fly indefinitely with constant speed, and the interference of gravitational force is ignored. Unlike the aforementioned fragmentation model, the number of fragments can be modified. The default value is 30 shrapnel in the beam of spray. A user can also define the type of shrapnel such as nails, bolts, screws etc. It is also assumed that the distribution of shrapnel in the explosive carrier is uniform.

In this model, shrapnel are not considered to be modeled individually, but rather as a single group. This means that the model does not allow individual shrapnel testing, but only calculates the total number of shrapnel in a given surface area on some distance i.e., density of fragments at a given range. With the implementation of blockage models discussed earlier, the simulation can identify parts of agents' bodies that will be impacted.

Equation 5.3 with Figure 5.7 describes the function used to calculate the density at given range [Kress 2004]:

$$\sigma_R = \frac{N}{4\pi R^2 \sin\dfrac{\beta}{2}} \cdot \qquad \text{Eq. 5.3}$$

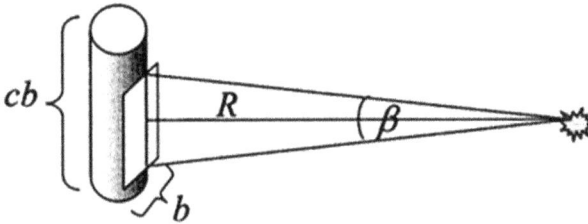

Figure 5.7. Shrapnel model by Moshe Kress [Kress 2004]

Where:

N = The number of fragments in the effective beam of spray

R = Range from bomber to person

b = diameter of the suicide belt

β = Dispersion angle (10 degrees).

5.3. Impact of Blockers on Severity of Injuries and Fragmentation

Table 5.3 gives an overview of the impact of full and partial blockers over injuries (as described in Chapter 3) and fragmentation. If a victim has a full blocker between him and the bomber, the blocker will reduce the blast overpressure by 20 peak overpressure PSI. This is in addition to the reduction in PSI due to the distance from the bomber. A partial blocker will reduce the PSI by 10 only.

Table 5.3. Impact of blockers on injuries and fragmentation.

	Full Blockers	**Partial Blockers**
Blast Overpressure	Reduced by 20 PSI	Reduced by 10 PSI
Fragmentation	Reduced to 0	Reduced by 10%

The total amount of reduction depends on the number of partial and full blockers one has between the bomber and himself. For fragmentation, a full blocker will consume all of the shrapnel from the bomber as a cookie-cutter function [Kress 2004], where a fragment or shrapnel can only injure at most one person. A partial blocker will reduce the number of fragments in the active beam-spray by 10%.

Suicide Bombing Database and Validation Scenarios

As part of this research we have compiled and continue to refine a real-life bombing and injuries database from the actual records of the suicide bombing incidents in Pakistan from November 15, 1995 to August 15th, 2009. The sources of data include local and international news channels and papers such as Daily Dawn, Daily Jang, and Daily Express News from Pakistan. Additionally, it also includes non-Pakistani news organizations such as CNN, BBC and Al-Jazeera. We have also used other sources such as MiPT terrorism repository, and have established links with Federal Intelligence Agency (FIA) of Pakistan, and various hospitals to gain and validate the data. We have included only those attacks that can be verified by at least two of the above mentioned sources. Readers are directed to our database portal (www.PakistanBodyCount.org) for complete set of data and casualty counts.

6. Suicide Bombing Database and Validation scenarios

6.1. The Database

As of August 15th 2009, Pakistan has experienced 189 suicide bombing attacks in 42 different cities that have left 2,508 dead and 6,381 injured. This study has compiled the records of the patients in most of these attacks. The records were obtained from the hospitals, which include patients' medico-legal reports, X-Rays, ECGs, PSTD profiles, injury types and characteristics. To the best of our knowledge, this database is the first of its kind in blast research on the human body.

Figure 6.1 presents a sample output of one of the incidents (Pakistan ordinance factory, Wah-Cantt, August 21, 2008) with scaled distance, weight (in kilograms) and age of the victims, that shows dead, minor and major injuries. Figure 6.2 shows a sample of a patients' medical record from the same incident. It shows that victims who are closer to the bomber have the higher chances of fatalities and major injuries.

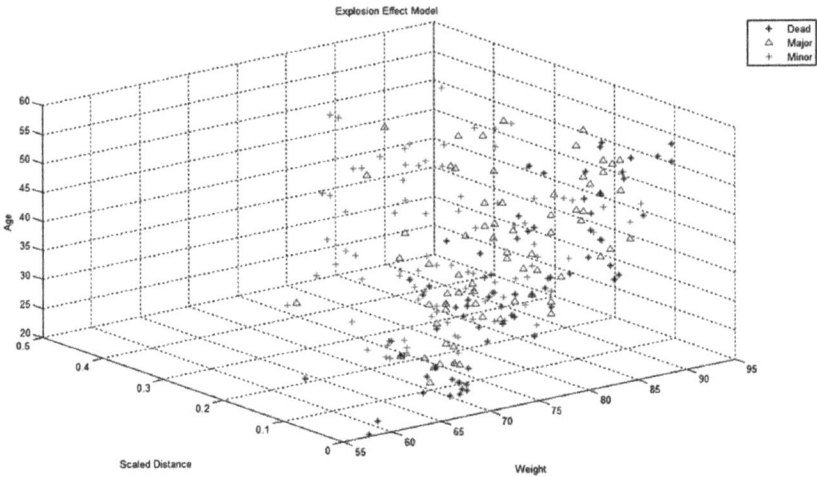

Figure 6.1. Suicide Bombing Injuries with Scaled Distance, Weight (kg), and Age.

S#	ML#	Name	Blast Date	Status	Age	Sex	Hospital	Wound	Length	Width	Diameter	Head	Neck	Upper Limb	Thorax	Abdomen	Lower Limb	Back	Pelvis & Perinium	Comments
			GENERAL INFORMATION						WOUND DETAIL						REGION INJURED					Comments
1	J-8369	Mohd. Asif	18.10.2007	Conscious	38	Male	Jinnah	Lacerated	3cm	1cm					R Chest					Skin deep and located in front
								Lacerated	2cm	0.5cm				R Arm						Skin deep
2	J-8371	Mohd. Ayub	18.10.2007	Conscious	36	Male	Jinnah	Lacerated	4cm	2cm						Abdomen				Muscle deep, right side (upper and lower was not mentioned)
								Lacerated	2cm	1cm							R Leg			Muscle deep
3	J-8372	Nabi Bux	18.10.2007	Conscious	22	Male	Jinnah	Lacerated	3cm	1cm		Head								Muscle deep on right cheek
								Lacerated	4cm	1cm				R Arm						Muscle deep
4	J-8374	Amjad Khan	18.10.2007	Conscious	10	Male	Jinnah	Lacerated	3cm	0.5cm							R Leg			Muscle deep
								Lacerated	2cm	0.5cm				R Arm						Muscle deep
5	J-8378	Mohd. Shahid	18.10.2007	Conscious	22	Male	Jinnah	Lacerated	4cm	4cm				L Arm						Muscle deep
								Lacerated	2cm	2cm				L Forearm						Muscle deep
6	J-8379	Mida Hussain	18.10.2007	Conscious	30	Male	Jinnah	Lacerated	3cm	2cm			Neck							Muscle deep located on right neck

Figure 6.2. Sample of Victims' Medical Record from the Database.

This study is mainly focused on open-space targets. This is due to fact that the majority of suicide bombing targets are in open-space like markets, streets and large gatherings. In a well-known manual of suicide bombing tactics by Al-Qaeeda, Al-Murqin describes the need and importance of bombings in urban and civilian targets with specific instructions for attacking a moving motorcade, market and restaurants [Al-Muqrin 2008]. Almost 70% of the victims in our database are between 15 and 30 years of age. This is in contrast to the findings of Limor where 50% of terrorism patients were between the age of 15-29 years or age, compared to other non-terrorism patients in trauma care [Limor and Shapira 2009].

6.2. Real-Life Scenarios from Pakistan

For the purpose of simulation and model validation, we have selected nine incidents from the database to compare and contrast the results. This is the first attempt to the best of our knowledge to test widely-used military and civilian models against actual real-life incidents of suicide bombing with human data. The selection of these nine incidents is based on the completeness of available data, since we would like to re-create the entire incident in our simulation software. The data include explosive characteristics such as weight and type of the bomb, weight and type of fragments that were being used, the height, weight, location, and orientation of the suicide bomber with respect to crowd and scenario geometry, distance and orientation of each victim to the bomber, number of human and non-human blockers available to each person and height, age, weight and gender of each victim in the scene. The complete dataset called *"Suicide Bombing in Pakistan – Dataset 1"* is available from the book website www.BlastSim.com

6.2.1. Scenario 1 – Lahore, Jamia Naeemia

On June 12, 2009, around 2:30 P.M just after Friday prayers at Jamia Neemia in the capital city of Punjab (Lahore), a suicide bomber blew himself up in the office (adjacent to the mosque) of Maulana Sarfaraz Naeemi. He was one of the six who was killed, five people were severely injured. Three sustained minor injuries, and seven sustained major injuries. The bomber was carrying 2 Kg of TNT equivalent of explosives with 0.5 kg of nuts and bolts tied together with the bomb as shrapnel. Figure 6.3 shows the simulation canvas of the scene, while Table 6.1 presents the age, weight, distance and the status of each victim in the arena.

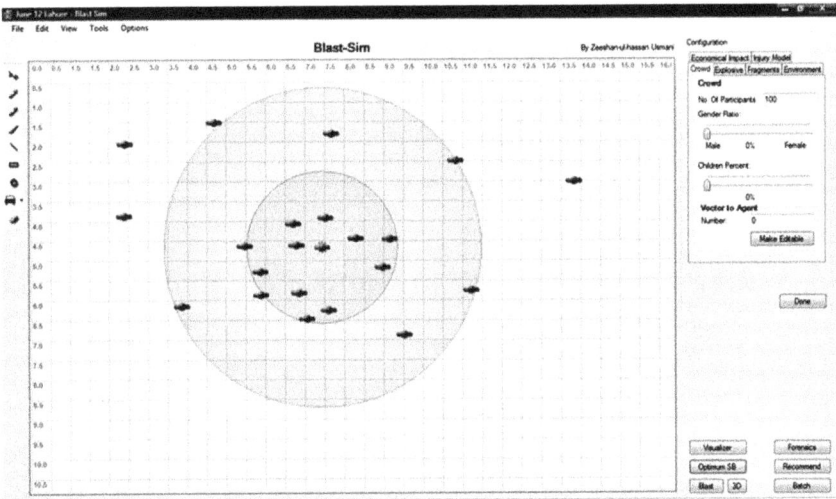

Figure 6.3. Suicide Bombing Simulation of Scenario 1.

Table 6.1. Data for Blast Victims of Scenario – 1.

S#	Age	Weight (Kg)	Distance (feet)	Status
1	20	58	3.1	Dead
2	21	60	2.1	Dead
3	21	68	5.2	Dead
4	22	62	2.5	Dead
5	23	67	2.9	Dead
6	23	68	4.2	Dead
7	23	69	5.3	Severe
8	24	69	5.7	Severe
9	24	68	6.0	Severe
10	24	68	6.4	Severe
11	25	68	6.5	Severe
12	25	68	5.5	Moderate
13	25	68	12.9	Moderate
14	26	70	9.9	Moderate
15	27	67	12.7	Minor
16	29	67	16.8	Minor
17	29	65	18.6	Minor
18	29	72	13.7	Minor
19	30	76	13.2	Minor
20	30	72	9.4	Minor
21	31	73	21.6	Minor

6.2.2. Scenario 2 – Wah-Cantt, Pakistan Ordinance Factory

On August 21, 2008, around 1:00 P.M, just after lunch break, two suicide bombers blew themselves up at the entrance of the Pakistan Ordinance Factory, Wah-Cantt, when laborers were coming out of the gates for their shift change. The bombers were carrying 10 and 12 Kg of TNT equivalents, respectively, with 1 kg of various shaped nails as shrapnel. The attack claimed the lives of 70 people, left 28 severely injured, 55 moderately injured, and 87 with minor injuries. The simulation canvas of the scene and the data table with the age, weight, distance and status of each victim in the arena is provided in the dataset. This incident is important for various reasons. First, it is the only event for which we have complete information where there were more than one suicide bomber, so the victims will receive blast overpressure from two different waves. Second, crowd density was very high since all of the laborers were trying to leave from the exits, and all victims were male with similar age range and physical characteristics. There were two suicide bombers in this scenario. The distance in the dataset refers to the closest distance from either of the bombers.

6.2.3. Scenario 3 – Muzaffarabad, Azad Jammu Kashmir

On June 26, 2009, at approximately 11:00 AM, a suicide bomber blew himself up near civilians in a city street. The bomber was carrying 2 Kg of TNT equivalent of explosives with 0.5 kg of screws tied together with the bomb as shrapnel. There were 14 people around that time, of which 2 were killed, 1 was severely injured, and 2 sustained minor injuries. The simulation canvas of the scene and the data table with the age, weight, distance and status of each victim in the arena is provided in the dataset available on book's website.

6.2.4. Scenario 4 – Marriott Hotel, Islamabad

On Jan 26, 2007, at approximately 2:35 P.M, a suicide bomber blew himself up outside the back gate of the Marriott hotel, Islamabad, near the laundry shop. The attack killed one security guard on duty, moderately injured 2 civilians and left 4 others with minor injuries. The bomber had 2 Kg of TNT strapped around his body with no added shrapnel. It is assumed that the explosion happened prematurely, by accident, while the motive of the bomber was to get inside the hotel premises. The simulation canvas of the scene and the data table with the age, weight, distance and status of each victim in the arena is provided in the dataset.

6.2.5. Scenario 5 – Islamabad Airport

On February 06, 2007, a suicide bomber ran from the airport entrance and headed directly towards the VIP lounge to target Prime Minister Shaukat

Aziz. The PM had left seconds ago, and the bomber was stopped again by a security guard when suddenly the bomb went off. The attack killed one security personnel, severely injured the other, and left 2 more passengers with moderate and minor injuries. The bomber had only 1 Kg of TNT, with 200 grams of screws and nails to be used as shrapnel. The simulation canvas of the scene and the data table with the age, weight, distance and status of each victim in the arena is provided in the dataset.

6.2.6. Scenario 6 – Aab-Para Market Restaurant

On July 27, 2007, at approximately 5:20 P.M, after a violent clash of protesters of Lal Masjid (Mosque) with police in the capital city of Pakistan (Islamabad), a suicide bomber targeted police personnel at a nearby restaurant (Muzaffargarh Nihari and Pakwan Center) at the Aab-Para market. The attack left 14 dead (including eight policemen), 12 severely injured, 15 with moderate injuries and 13 with minor injuries. The bomber was carrying approximately 5 Kg of TNT equivalent and 1 Kg of shrapnel. The simulation canvas of the scene and the data table with the age, weight, distance and status of each victim in the arena is provided in the dataset.

6.2.7. Scenario 7 – ISI Bus, Rawalpindi

On September 4, 2007, a suicide bomber attacked a government transport bus at the Qasim Market, near R. A. Bazar, that was carrying staff members of the Inter Service Intelligence (ISI) of Pakistan. The attack killed 23 officials, severely injured 27, moderately injured 16, and left 15 with minor injuries. The bomber was carrying 8 Kg of TNT with 3 Kg of added bolts as shrapnel. This incidence is unique since it happened in a confined-space. Typically, there is more damage in confined-space explosions as compare to those in open-spaces. The simulation canvas of the scene and the data table with the age, weight, distance and status of each victim in the arena is provided in the dataset.

6.2.8. Scenario 8 – Isfandyar Wali House

On October 1st, 2008, at approximately 10:00 A.M, a suicide bomber blew himself up at the security checkpoint of the main gate of provincial minister Isfadyar Wali Khan. The attack killed 5 persons, severely injured 9, moderately injured 3, and left 4 with minor injuries. The bomber had 4 Kg of TNT strapped around his body with 1.5 Kg of added shrapnel. The simulation canvas of the scene and the data table with the age, weight, distance and status of each victim in the arena is provided in the dataset.

6.2.9. Scenario 9 – Joint Chief of Army Staff, Rawalpindi

On October 30, 2007, at approximately 9:00 A.M, a suicide bomber attacked at the house of Joint Chief of Army Staff in Rawalpindi. The attack killed eight persons, severely injured 7, moderately injured another 7, and left 5 with minor injuries. The bomber had 4 Kg of TNT strapped around his body with 2 Kg of added shrapnel. The target was the Joint Chief of Army Staff, but security personnel tried to stop him at the front gate of the house. The bomber tried to run into the house and when stopped again by security, he detonated the explosion. The simulation canvas of the scene and the data table with the age, weight, distance and status of each victim in the arena is provided in the dataset.

6.2.10. Scenario 10 – Benazir Bhutto

On December 27, 2007, at approximately 6:00 P.M, a suicide bomber carrying 20 Kg of TNT equivalent, with 2 Kg of added shrapnel, attacked the rally of former Prime Minister Benazir Bhutto. The bomber killed the former Prime Minister with 31 others, and left 33 severely injured. Another 34 persons sustained moderate injuries, and 33 sustained minor injuries. This situation is unique, because the listed data is publicly available on the internet. We do not know, however, the characteristics of the explosive being used, the crowd formation pattern, and total number of people in the arena. We want to simulate this incident to see how well the model performs on random situation or when we don't have much data.

7. BlastSim Simulation Framework

The effects of an explosion are contingent upon various factors, such as: explosive type (i.e. TNT, RDX, C4, AN etc.), explosive weight and its respective peak overpressure, ignition source and criteria, crowd density (number of people per square meter), crowd demographics (i.e. age, gender, weight, height), pulse duration, reflection waves, living and non-living blockage, size, shape, location, number of obstacles, projectiles, debris and fragments, and shape of the explosive carrier. A suicide bombing model and simulation should consider all of these factors. Furthermore, the model should be easy to use, contain appropriate physics, be able to work with different scenarios, blockage ratios, injury matrices and different ambient conditions without special time-consuming tuning of parameters. The model should also have sufficient numerical accuracy to allow realistic representation of geometry and explosive strength. It should be easy to configure, and execute in a short amount of time.

Some of these requirements are contradictory. For example, a complex model will require too many resources and time if it truly contains appropriate physics and complex geometries. Consequently, a good model should allow for a tradeoff among time, resources, physics, geometry and the resulting output. Sometimes there is a need for faster results to be able to save lives, and sometimes there are scarce resources to distribute for various purposes. A good model should be flexible enough to use in a diverse set of situations with varying requirements. BlastSim framework is fulfilling this gap by providing faster results while taking care of all the required characteristics of a good model.

7.1. Modeling Approach

Authors have developed a comprehensive framework called BlastSim, to predict the damage of a suicide bombing attack as illustrated in Figure 7.1.

The main goal of our research is to program and define a general blast wave explosion model to predict and estimate the damage for such incidents with various crowd and explosive characteristics. The BlastSim is physics based stationary multi-agent simulation platform to model and simulate a suicide bombing event. The agents are constrained by the physical characteristics and mechanics of the blast wave. The BlastSim is programmed to test, analyze, and validate the results of different model combinations under various conditions with different sets of parameters, such as the crowd and explosive characteristics, blockage and human shields, fragmentation and the bomber's position, in 2-dimensional and 3-dimensional environments. The proposed framework will be a total turn-key solution for emergency response management, casualty prediction, classification of injuries, and will provide a safe distance matrix to event managers and security officials. The framework is general enough and based on publicly available information to make it unclassified (thus avoiding misuse) and specific enough to give an educated guess for the outcome.

The framework has following four main components:

1. **Explosive Models:** This component provides widely used explosion models to estimate the blast peak overpressure at any given distance from the bomber. A user can select the model of his/her choice based on the situation with which he/she is dealing. For example, if we have to model an open-space situation we would take *Harold Brode* model to do the estimations, *JClutter with Reflection* model will be more suitable for confined-space explosions like a suicide bombing attack on a bus, or *US Army* model works best for least conservative estimates. The details and properties of these models were discussed in Chapter 3.

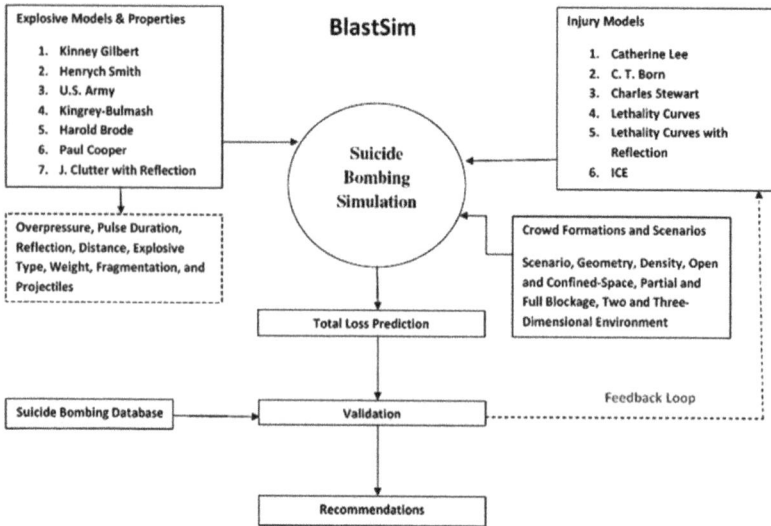

Figure 7.1. Components of the BlastSim suicide bombing model: (1) Explosion modeling, (2) Quantification of crowd formation, (3) Model to predict casualty and injury level, and (4) Database for model validation.

2. **Injury Models:** This component provides one of the widely used injury models to map the peak overpressure PSI to human injuries. A user can also select all models to have a comparative view and range of predictions by all of the models to have a better guess.

3. **Crowd Formations and Scenarios:** This component helps the user to define and draw the scenario over the BlastSim canvas. A user can pick environmental properties, assign two-dimensional and three-dimensional constants, city temperature and altitude, crowd density, gender, age, height and number of children, and can also form a particular formation like row-wise or zig-zag to distribute the crowd. The set of tools available in this component can help the user to re-create the actual event for forensics analysis.

4. **Suicide Bombing Database:** This component provides the historical information about actual suicide bombing incidents in Pakistan, with painstaking details of victims, injuries, explosive and crowd characteristics. The benefits of this component are twofold. First it provides the necessary data to simulate the event,

and then the results of the simulation can be validated against the database for accuracy and estimates.

7.2. Simulation Tool Development

The simulation is being programmed in Visual C# 2005. Visual C# was used due to its extensive library of graphics and geometry functions (to generate the Cartesian grid with agents) and exceptional coverage of code integration with other third party tools like MatLab® (to code the blast overpressure and explosion models). In the simulation, it is assumed that the crowd is uniformly distributed throughout the area. The explosive range is determined by one of the explosion models described earlier in Chapter 3. It is easy to calculate the exact overpressure received by each agent at particular locations given the weight and type of explosive. Specific simulation inputs are the number of individuals and bombers in the vicinity, explosive characteristics (type, weight, fragmentation etc.), and crowd formation (topology, gender, height, width, weight etc). Additionally the arrival time of the explosive pressure front to travel from the point of explosion to any given location may also be calculated. Furthermore, user can also define environment, and three-dimensional parameters.

The work has only considered primary and secondary injuries. Persons who are directly in the line-of-sight with an explosion will absorb the effects, and thus act as a shield for person(s) behind them. Direct injuries mean injuries caused by the bomb's blast wave overpressure during the explosion, and not by fire or debris (pieces of furniture or glass). Secondary injuries are usually caused by flying pieces of fragments and shrapnel. The work does not incorporate tertiary injuries at this point of time – injuries caused by toxic poisoning, whole body translation, and building or structural collapse.

The work has also considered mostly "open space" scenarios to serve as the basis for our crowd formation types (e.g., mosques, streets, concerts etc.). The types of injury caused by overpressure depend on whether overpressure occurs in open or confined space. In the later case the type of injuries also depends on whether the explosion causes collapse of a building or other structure. There are numerous objects to consider in closed environments that can either increase the casualty/injury toll (primarily by working as flying debris) or decrease the toll by providing a shield to humans. Closed environments also need to entertain reflection waves. A blast wave can amplify in closed environments by reflection and reduced ventilation. The simulation has *"JClutter with Reflection"* model to take care of confined-space explosions.

There are basically two types of formations a user can choose from – random formations and user created scenarios, like circles, zigzags, rectangular etc to represent real-life settings like cafeteria, mosques, concerts etc. – to estimate the outcome of an attack for a particular crowd formation. The simulation takes care of beam and line-of-sight adjustments in cases of uneven surfaces (e.g., concert stage, mosque or shopping mall). A suicide bomber is a pedestrian in all cases and the explosion does not originate from a moving vehicle. A user can place the suicide bomber wherever he wants on the canvas, but as witnessed by recent attacks in Iraq, Israel and Pakistan where suicide bombers detonated at the gates of mosques and restaurants, it is more realistic to place the bomber near or on the entrance or exit gates if the user does not have the information about the bomber's location [Johnson 2000].

Figure 7.2 shows an interesting example of a simulation scenario, where two seemingly similar formations – both have the same minimum average distance from the bomber – can lead to a totally different lethality and injury results.

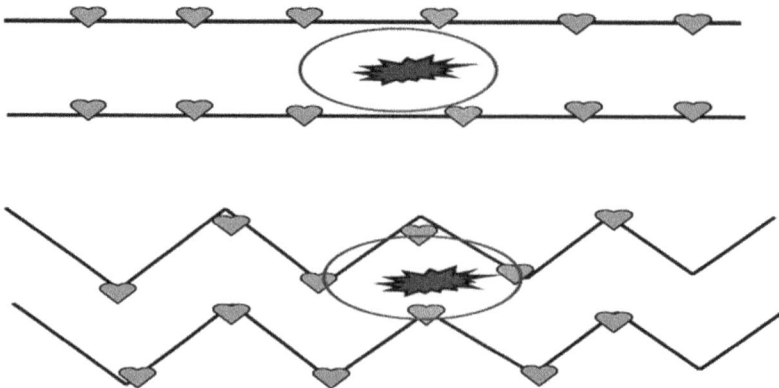

Figure 7.2: An Example Impact of Crowd Formation on Casualty Count.

In the row wise formation there is no person directly in the range of the blast zone, while in the zigzag fashion, there are at least four persons directly in the blast zone, thus reducing their chances of survival. Partial or full blockage (as described in Chapter 5) can further complicate the situation, and consequently the assessment.

8. Results

The overall goal of this chapter is to compare, contrast and analyze the performance of explosive and injury models against the real-life incidents' data described in chapter 7. We describe a simulation tool, BlastSim, which provides a platform to test, analyze, and validate the results of different model combinations under various conditions with different set of parameters, e.g., crowd and explosive characteristics, blockage and human shields, and an option of 2-dimensional and 3-dimensional environment. Furthermore, this chapter also presents a sample statistical analysis that can be performed on the data generated by the simulation.

There are five main sections in this chapter. Section 8.1 discusses the overall setup in which the results have been generated and also provides the list of proposed models and combinations. Section 8.2 provides a glimpse and re-cap of the real-life data used to compare the models. Section 8.3 reveals a list of appraisal functions to compare, contrast and analyze the results and performance of individual models for various purposes. Section 8.4 is the main section that presents results, charts and analysis of BlastSim simulation runs and performance. The chapter concludes in Section 8.5 with a brief summary and limitations of the study.

8.1. BlastSim Setup

All models were executed on the exact same data. This includes 9 real-life incidents, and a random case (scenario 10) as explained in the Chapter 6. Table 8.1 lists all 27 models. The same numbering scheme (1-27) has been used throughout the text for model identification. For example, model 1 will always refer to Kinney Gilbert's explosion model along with Catherine Lee's Injury model (as described respectively in Chapter 3 and 4), and so on. There are seven explosive models and six injury models in total. All of the injury models cannot be used with all of the explosive models due to incompatibilities between input-output parameters. The given list of 27 models represents all *possible* combinations. We have also performed additional runs for sensitivity analysis. Although the data we received for each scenario has been validated by at least four different sources (as described in Chapter 6), nonetheless we have run the simulation for ±3 feet of distance for each victim from the explosion, ±2 Kg of TNT for each explosion, and two distinct perturbation of crowd orientation (perpendicular and parallel to the bomber).

The 10 scenarios used in this simulation were chosen because they represent many real situations. They were picked after careful investigation, authentication, and to have a diverse set of test inputs. For example, scenario 1 contains no human blockage, and almost every person is in direct-line-of-sight with the bomber. Scenario 2 has the highest crowd density, and thus the greater human blockage available, while scenario 7 contains a suicide bombing incident in a confined-space (a bus). It would help us to distinguish the models that work best for each type of scenario. A model that yields the best estimates for a higher density crowd may not be an appropriate choice for a crowd with fewer than 20 people. Similarly a model that gives better results for an open-space incident may not be the perfect match for a confined-space scenario. We may not find "the best" model for all possible situations, but a set of models that can be used based on situation and environment. The results can also lead to a scientific scaling between open-space and confined-space scenarios, or a count-multiplier based on the crowd density.

Table 8.1. Simulation Models.

Model #	Explosion Model	Injury Model
1	Kinney Gilbert	Catherine Lee
2	Kinney Gilbert	C. T. Born
3	Kinney Gilbert	Charles Stewart
4	Henrych Smith	Catherine Lee
5	Henrych Smith	C. T. Born
6	Henrych Smith	Charles Stewart

Model #	Explosion Model	Injury Model
7	U.S. Army	Catherine Lee
8	U.S. Army	C. T. Born
9	U.S. Army	Charles Stewart
10	Kingrey Bulmash	Catherine Lee
11	Kingrey Bulmash	C. T. Born
12	Kingrey Bulmash	Charles Stewart
13	Harold Brode	Catherine Lee
14	Harold Brode	C. T. Born
15	Harold Brode	Charles Stewart
16	Harold Brode	Lethality Curves
17	Harold Brode	Lethality Curved with Reflection
18	Harold Brode	ICE
19	Paul Cooper	Catherine Lee
20	Paul Cooper	C. T. Born
21	Paul Cooper	Charles Stewart
22	**Paul Cooper**	**Lethality Curves**
23	Paul Cooper	Lethality Curved with Reflection
24	Paul Cooper	ICE
25	Jclutter with Reflection	Catherine Lee
26	Jclutter with Reflection	C. T. Born
27	Jclutter with Reflection	Charles Stewart

It should be noted that majority of the proposed model combinations are totally new. For example, all models with direct blast overpressure to human injury mapping, such as Catherine Lee, Charles Stewart and C. T. Born, were derived from medical literature. These models have not been used previously in blast loading, mechanical engineering, or in simulation and modeling. The best, newest, and widely accepted model available for this kind of simulation is Model # 22 (Paul Cooper with Bowen's Lethality Curves). Comparison with Model 22 will thus provide a good benchmark for comparing the proposed model and simulation to the state-of-the-art simulation and modeling of blast to predict injuries and lethality.

To compare and contrast the performance of all models over the given scenario we need an appraisal function to weight the predictions. An appraisal function is a yardstick to compare given models and their results. An appraisal function can be biased to favor one set of results or model over another. Sometimes there is also a need to bias an appraisal function. For example, a dead or severely injured person should have more "value" than a person with minor injuries in the simulation count. More specifically, if a dead or severely injured person is not counted, resources for that missing person, whether it is reserving an ambulance, additional blood or medical supplies, or simply finding another body under the debris, will not be estimated correctly. Similarly, overlooking a person who only had some bruises and walked home on his feet might not be that important.

We have quite a few models that provide good results only if we compare the total victims (including all dead, severe, moderate and minor injured), but perform poorly when it comes to separate the victims based on intensity of their condition. For example, if we have 80 dead people and 0 injured in the actual event, a model that predicts 70 dead, and 10 injured should be valued more than a model that predicts 10 dead, and 70 injured. For this reason, we have a weight factor that penalizes the model based on the severity of injury, i.e., a dead count equals 1, severe injured equals 0.75, moderate injured equals 0.50, and minor injured weighs only 0.25 of the actual count.

8.2. *Suicide Bombing Data*

Table 8.2 provides the counts for dead, major, moderate and minor injured in 10 real-life incidents (details are given in Chapter 6 and the dataset available on book's website). These numbers are referred to as Model 0 in the simulation results, and the ones to when we are comparing the output of all the models. We have picked these scenarios on the basis of the completeness of data we needed to re-create these incidents in the simulation, for example, explosive weight, type, bomber's position and distance of each person from the bomber. The scenarios are diverse, for example, the scenario 1 has no crowd blockage, the scenario 2 has the highest crowd blockage (these two scenarios were picked to measure the impact of out proposed blockage model). The scenario 7 on the other hand represents an explosion in confined space (an SB attack in a bus), and the scenario 8 happens with a building collapse. With all these different situations, we are expecting quite a few different model combinations to predict the best results.

Table 8.2. Real-life actual counts of victims.

Scenario #	Dead	Injured			Total
		Major	Moderate	Minor	
1	6	5	3	7	21
2	70	28	55	87	240
3	2	1	1	1	5
4	1	0	2	4	7
5	1	1	1	1	4
6	14	12	15	13	54
7	23	27	16	15	81
8	5	9	3	4	21
9	8	7	7	5	27
10	32	33	34	34	133

There is a difference of opinion on how to rank a person for severe, moderate and minor injuries. A person with few fragments can be easily classified as either minor, moderate or severely injured based on the location, size, and intensity of the injury, as well as on the experience and knowledge of the doctor treating the victim. We have followed the triage criteria (described in Chapter 4 – Blast Injuries) used by the W.H.O (World Health Organization) and the U.N. (United Nations). A minor injured in one model will therefore have the same level of criticality compared to a minor injured in another model. The difference lies in how the victim gets there, as one model would place him with, for example, 20 PSI of overpressure, while another might place him with 50 PSI, but once inside the *Minor Injured* category, the severity of an injury means the same.

Figure 8.1 reveals the distribution of injuries and lethality counts in all 10 incidents. As shown in the Figure, on average 1/4 of the victims are dead. An almost similar percentage of the persons is in the minor injury zone. Similarly, major and moderate injuries take an almost equal number of shares. As described above, scenario 2, which has the highest crowd density, placed almost half of the victims (11.67 Vs. 23.81) in the major injury bracket compared to the scenario 1. In contrast, with almost the same level of crowd density, scenario 7 left 33.33% of the people in major injured. Intuitively this makes sense due to the confined-space nature of the explosion in Scenario 7. It is safe to say that one can expect three times more major injuries in a confined-space explosion compared to one in an otherwise comparable open-space. We will revisit this figure at the end of this chapter, and will compare it against the best-performing models.

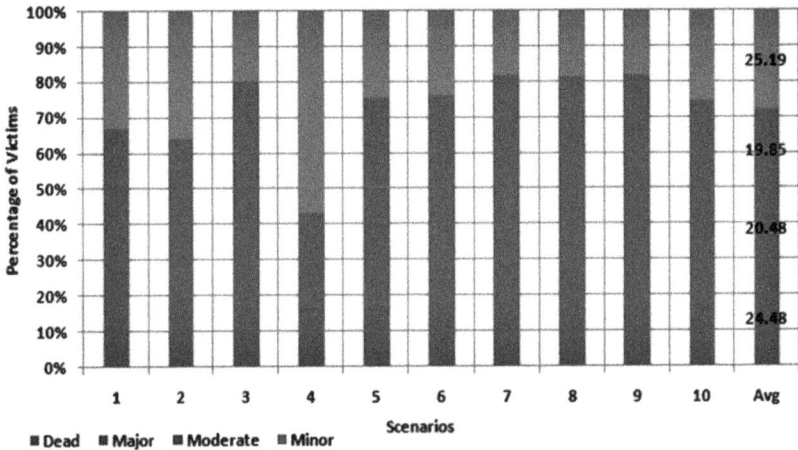

Figure 8.1: Distribution of Injuries in Real-Life Counts.

8.3. *BlastSim Appraisal Functions*

To compare and contrast the models against Model 0 (the real-life benchmark data), and among other models, this section gives a set of scoring methods as appraisal functions. Which appraisal function is used depends on the type of analysis one needs for a particular situation. For example, one might be interested in only the severely and moderately injured people, so resources can be directed to save lives. Since there is nothing that can be done for already dead persons, and since minor victims can walk by themselves to nearby medical care facilities, the people who are of great importance are those with major and moderate injuries. In this particular case, one needs an appraisal function that points out the best model for predicting the severely and moderately injured persons.

In another case, for example, an event manger might want to re-arrange a crowd in such a way that reduces the number of deaths. In this case, an appraisal function bias towards dead would be more beneficial to determine an appropriate model. There could be literally dozens of appraisal and scoring methods that can be defined for this set of data. Table 8.3 provides a list of scoring methods, their brief descriptions, list of formulae, and gives an example of a how an appraisal function can be used for immediate comparison, for most of the common-sense cases and analyses.

Table 8.3. Appraisal Functions (subscript 0 always refers to real-life counts).

Method	Description	Type	Formula
Score 1a	Weighted Absolute	Absolute	$Score1a = \|Dead - Dead_0\| + \frac{4}{5}\|Major - Major_0\| + \frac{3}{5}\|Interm - Interm_0\| + \frac{1}{5}\|Minor - Minor_0\|$
Score 1r	Difference wrt Model 0	Relative	$Score1r = \frac{\|Dead - Dead_0\|}{Dead_0} + \frac{4}{5}\frac{\|Major - Major_0\|}{Major_0} + \frac{3}{5}\frac{\|Moderate - Moderate_0\|}{Moderate_0} + \frac{1}{5}\frac{\|Minor - Minor_0\|}{Minor_0}$
Score 1rr		Accuracy	$Score1rr = 1 - \frac{\|Dead - Dead_0\| + \frac{4}{5}\|Major - Major_0\| + \frac{3}{5}\|Moderate - Moderate_0\| + \frac{1}{5}\|Minor - Minor_0\|}{Dead_0 + \frac{4}{5}Major_0 + \frac{3}{5}Moderate_0 + \frac{1}{5}Minor_0}$
Score 2a	Dead Count Difference wrt	Absolute	$Score2a = \|Dead - Dead_0\|$
Score 2r	Model 0	Relative	$Score2r = \frac{\|Dead - Dead_0\|}{Dead_0}$
Score 2rr		Accuracy	$Score2rr = 1 - \frac{\|Dead - Dead_0\|}{Dead_0}$
Score 3a	Major Injury Difference wrt	Absolute	$Score3a = \|Major - Major_0\|$
Score 3r	Model 0	Relative	$Score3r = \frac{\|Major - Major_0\|}{Major_0}$
Score 3rr		Accuracy	$Score3rr = 1 - \frac{\|Major - Major_0\|}{Major_0}$
Score 4a	Weighted Difference wrt	Absolute	$Score4a = \|Dead - Dead_0\| + \frac{2}{3}\|Major - Major_0\| + \frac{1}{3}\|Moderate - Moderate_0\|$
Score 4r	Model 0 (not incl. Minor	Relative	$Score4r = \frac{\|Dead - Dead_0\|}{Dead_0} + \frac{2}{3}\frac{\|Major - Major_0\|}{Major_0} + \frac{1}{3}\frac{\|Moderate - Moderate_0\|}{Moderate_0}$
Score 4rr	Injuries)	Accuracy	$Score4rr = 1 - \frac{\|Dead - Dead_0\| + \frac{2}{3}\|Major - Major_0\| + \frac{1}{3}\|Moderate - Moderate_0\|}{Dead_0 + \frac{2}{3}Major_0 + \frac{1}{3}Moderate_0}$
Score 5a	Total Count Difference wrt	Absolute	$Score5a = \|Dead + Major + Moderate + Minor - Dead_0 - Major_0 - Moderate_0 - Minor_0\|$
Score 5r	Model 0	Relative	$Score5r = \left\|\frac{Dead + Major + Moderate + Minor}{Dead_0 + Major_0 + Moderate_0 + Minor_0} - 1\right\|$
Score 5rr		Accuracy	$Score5rr = 1 - \left\|\frac{Dead + Major + Moderate + Minor}{Dead_0 + Major_0 + Moderate_0 + Minor_0} - 1\right\|$
Score 6a	Euclidian Weighted	Absolute	$Score6a = \sqrt{(Dead - Dead_0)^2 + (\frac{4}{5}(Major - Major_0))^2 + (\frac{3}{5}(Moderate - Moderate_0))^2 + (\frac{1}{5}(Minor - Minor_0))^2}$
Score 6r	Difference wrt Model 0	Relative	$Score6r = \sqrt{\left(\frac{Dead - Dead_0}{Dead_0}\right)^2 + \frac{4}{5}\left(\frac{Major - Major_0}{Major_0}\right)^2 + \frac{3}{5}\left(\frac{Moderate - Moderate_0}{Moderate_0}\right)^2 + \frac{1}{5}\left(\frac{Minor - Minor_0}{Minor_0}\right)^2}$
Score 6rr		Accuracy	$Score6rr = 1 - \frac{\sqrt{(Dead - Dead_0)^2 + (\frac{4}{5}(Major - Major_0))^2 + (\frac{3}{5}(Moderate - Moderate_0))^2 + (\frac{1}{5}(Minor - Minor_0))^2}}{\sqrt{Dead_0^2 + (\frac{4}{5}Major_0)^2 + (\frac{3}{5}Moderate_0)^2 + (\frac{1}{5}Minor_0)^2}}$

8.3.1. Score 1 – Weighted Absolute Difference wrt Model 0

In the *Weighted Absolute Difference wrt Model 0 (Score 1)*, the following penalty/weight system has been used for each count to bias the results towards counts with more critical injuries and dead:

- 1 per difference in dead count,
- 0.75 per difference in major injury count
- 0.5 per difference in moderate injury count·
- 0.25 per difference in moderate injury count

The importance of dead is therefore 4 times higher than a minor injured. The final score is given either as the sum of the weighted absolute differences, or as a ratio of the absolute difference to the actual case. On the whole, the first method (Score 1a) grants higher leverage to scenarios with high casualties. The second method (Score 1r) offers a kind of "normalization" of the data so that equal importance is given to scenarios with high or low casualties. Table 8.4 presents an example of scores using this method.

Table 8.4. Example of Score 1.

	Dead	Major	Moderate	Minor
Real-life count (Scenario # 01)	6	5	3	7
Model # 7 Output	9	3	2	6
Absolute Difference	3	2	1	1
Weighted Absolute Difference	3	1.5	0.5	0.25
Score (Absolute) **(Score 1a)**	5.25			
Weighted Score of Real-life count	6	3.75	1.5	1.75
	13			
Accuracy **(Score 1rr)**	59.6%			
Ratio of Weighted Absolute Difference to Real-life count	0.5	0.3	0.16667	0.03571
Score Relative **(Score 1r)**	1.00238			

These two methods measure the gap between the given model and the actual case. It is also convenient to define a relative accuracy measure that stems from the previous ones: 1 (i.e., 100%) corresponds to a perfect match to the actual case, decreasing to 0 as the results drift away from the actual case.

8.3.2. Score 2 – Dead Count Difference wrt Model 0

Given the high importance of the dead count for the appraisal of the models, this information alone is regarded as a scoring method, either as an absolute count, or as a ratio with respect to the actual dead count. In the example above, the absolute score of model #7 would be 3, and the relative score would be 0.5.

8.3.3. Score 3 – Major Injury Difference wrt Model 0

This method can be used where the major injury count is of primary interest. In the example above, the absolute score of model #7 would be 2, and the relative score would be 0.4.

8.3.4. Score 4 – Weighted Difference wrt Model 0 (not including Minor Injuries)

Although some models accurately predict the dead count and the severe injury count, they may have very poor performance in predicting minor injuries. With the first scoring method, in spite of a factor of 4 between dead count and minor injury count, it may end up with a bad ranking. These models could nonetheless be useful. In some scenarios we therefore provide a specific scoring method that does not take into account the gap in prediction of minor injuries. In the example above, model #7 would be granted an absolute score of 5 (5.25-0.25), and a relative score of 0.96667 (1.00238-0.03571).

8.3.5. Score 5 – Total Count Difference wrt Model 0

This scoring method is the un-weighted equivalent of the first method; a miss of 1 person in the dead count or any injury count gives the same penalty. In the example, the score of model #7 would be 1 in absolute value, and 4.762 in relative value.

8.3.6. Score 6 – Euclidian Weighted Difference wrt Model 0

This scoring method leads to quite a different way of comparing models against each other. Whereas previous methods granted an equal penalty for each person missed with respect to the actual case, in this case, the higher the miss, the higher the penalty per missed person (squared difference). Table 8.5 revisits the example presented in Table 8.4 in terms of Euclidean difference.

Table 8.5. Example of Score 6.

	Dead	Major	Moderate	Minor
Real-life count (Scenario # 01)	6	5	3	7
Model # 7 Output	9	3	2	6
Signed Difference	3	-2	-1	-1
Weighted Signed Difference	3	-1.5	-0.5	-0.25
Squared Weighted Difference	9	2.25	0.25	0.0625
Score (Absolute) **(Score 6a)**	3.4004			
Weighted Score of Real-life count	36	18.75	4.5	12.25
	8.45577			
Accuracy **(Score 6rr)**	59.6%			
Ratio of Weighted Signed Difference to Real-life count	0.5	-0.3	-0.16667	-0.03571
Squared Ratio of Weighted Difference to Actual Case	0.25	0.09	0.02778	$1.2755. \ 10^{-3}$
Score Relative **(Score 6r)**	0.6075			

With this example, we can see that scoring methods 1 & 6 yield quite similar results. We will primarily be using scoring method 6 in the rest of the chapter for our discussions. However, charts can be generated with all scoring methods and types for readers interested in specific scoring methods.

8.4. *Interpretation of Scores*

This section describes how to interpret the scores. The definition remains the same for all scoring methods (1 to 6).

- **Absolute Score:** The closer to 0, the better, where 0 represents the score of the actual real-life count. For all scoring methods, each score unit represents a gap of one person with respect to the actual case, weighted differently depending on the method. For instance, if a model scores 6 with method #5, this means that the median total count of this model is higher or lower by 6 persons with respect to the total count of the actual case.

- **Relative Score:** The closer to 0, the better, where 0 corresponds to an exact match to the actual case on a specific criterion defined by the scoring method. With the same example, if a model scores 0.2 with method #5, this means that the total count is 20% higher or lower with respect to the total count of the actual case.

- **Accuracy:** Accuracy is nothing more than a different way to express relative score. Basically, relative score is a measure of the inaccuracy of a model. Here, the closer to 1 (i.e. 100%), the better. 100% is an exact match with the actual case on the considered criterion. When accuracy decreases to 0%, this means that the model's error in the estimation is at least equal to the actual case.

8.5. *Analysis of BlastSim Model Performance*

This section presents the simulation results. The results were compared with the scoring methods described in the Section 8.3. The following sub-sections provide each model's performance based on a scenario, scoring method, blockage, crowd density and the sensitivity analysis.

8.5.1. Data Scatter

There is an enormous scattering of data among different scenarios for the total victim count. Figure 8.2 shows that scenarios 2, 6, and 7 have high leverage for all scoring methods. These scenarios have first order effect on the model ranking. These differences will be leveled down when using the relative score. However, since the model output is integral, even a miss of one count can significantly change the results.

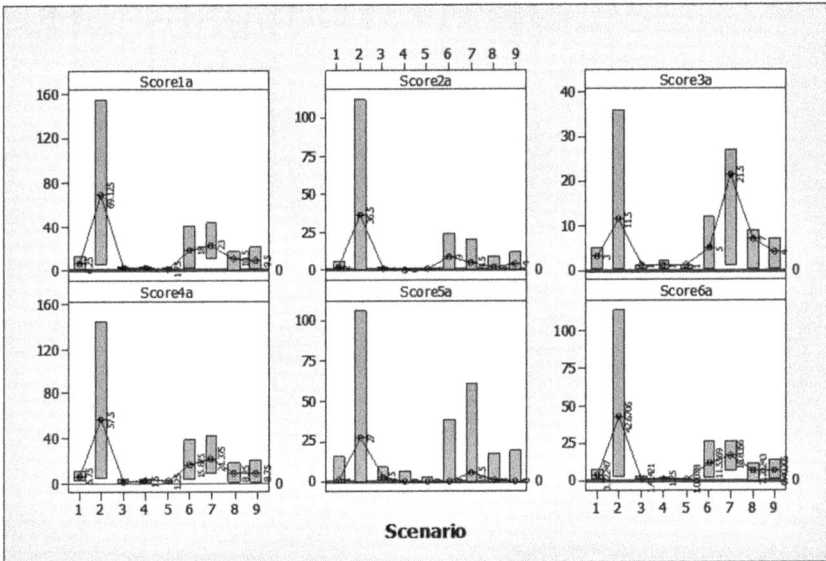

Figure 8.2. Scattering of Data Points in each Scenario by all Scoring Methods.

8.5.2. Performance Assessment Model by Model

This section presents a model-by-model performance assessment using BoxPlots. Figure 8.3 provides an immediate visual synthesis using aggregate scoring. The yellow bar represents range, and the cross-box represents the median values. In this sub-section, all results are given with the blockage algorithm, as discussed in Chapter 5 – Blockage and Fragmentation. In addition, all scenarios have equal importance. Model 13 shows the best cumulative performance on all scenarios, with an accuracy percentage of 87.6%. This is an overwhelming 71% improvement in accuracy compare to the widely used Model 22, with 15.7% cumulative accuracy percentage. Model 24 comes in last with an almost 0% cumulative accuracy.

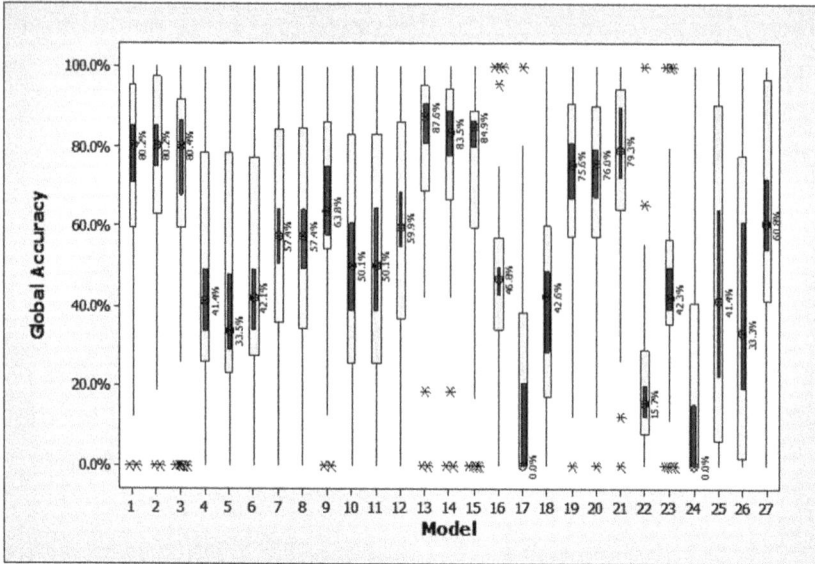

Figure 8.3. Cumulative Performance of all Models over all Scenarios using Aggregate Score.

For the same analysis, Score 3 (only major injuries) shows a large number of outliers. The bad performance mainly comes from scenario 7 (confined-space special case), where a majority of the models failed to predict the number of injuries by a large margin. The median prediction is 6, compared to the actual count of 27. Overall, models #13 and #15 obtained the best performance with 84.4% median accuracy. This is a 73% increase compared to Model 22.

8.5.3. Performance Assessment Scenario by Scenario

This section presents a few examples of the cumulative performance of all models on individual scenarios using aggregate scoring. Figure 8.4 presents the results of model performance on scenario 1. All of the Harold Brode models with direct human injury mapping yield the best results with 82.3% accuracy. Since there is very little blockage available in the crowd, the results remain the same with and without the use of a blockage model. Reflection models perform the worst on scenario 1, since there are generally no reflection waves in open-space scenarios. Model 17 (using Bowen's lethality curve reflection injury model) and Model 24 (with J. Clutter explosion reflection model) yield almost 0% accuracy. Model 22 was able to give only 3.3% accuracy. The best models (13 to 15) were 79% better in injury estimates. This trend remains consistent for the rest of the scenarios. The best accuracy percentage given by Model 22 for any scenario was 32%, still far behind the best performing models.

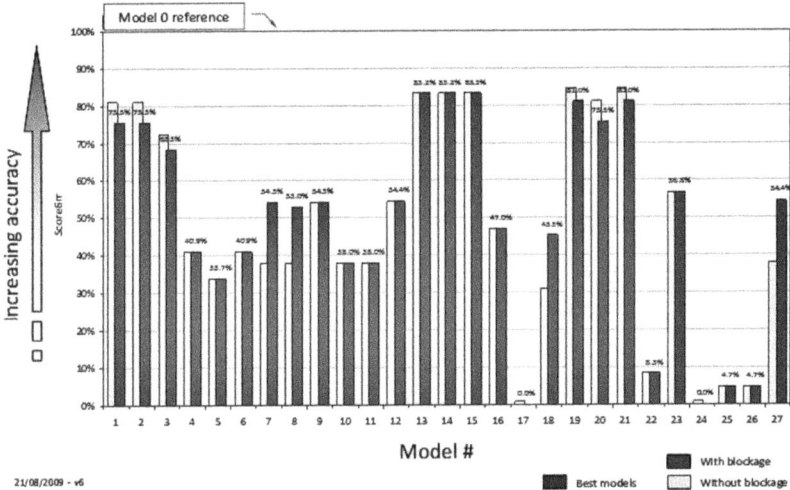

Figure 8.4. Models Cumulative Scoring Performance on Scenario 1.

Figure 8.5 presents model performance on Scenario 2. As described earlier, this scenario has the maximum number of blockers in the crowd. Model 13 gains an enormous 46% increase in accuracy (using blockage model for this crowd) with an overall accuracy of 96.2%. Model 22 trails behind with 49.3% accuracy. This figure clearly shows the importance of considering blockage in the crowd and shows that statistically significant improvement can be made using a blockage model.

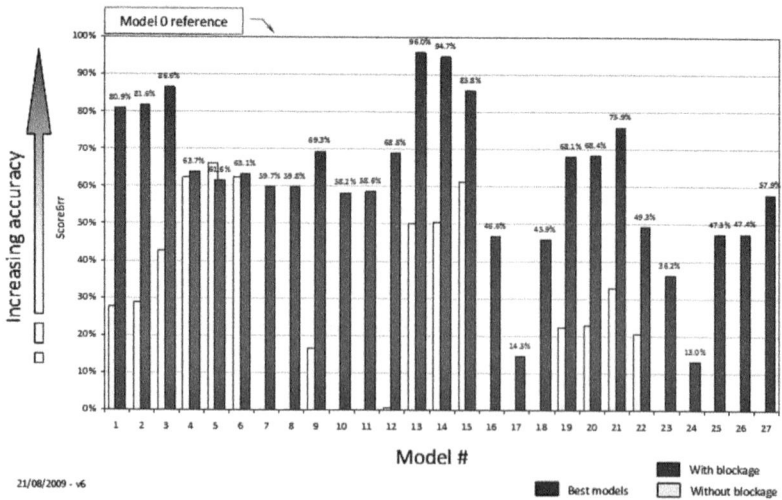

Figure 8.5. Models Cumulative Scoring Performance on Scenario 2.

Figure 8.6 portrays model performance on Scenario 7. Unexpectedly, our best performing models (13 to 15) show poor performance on this scenario. This is not surprising since scenario 7 is an example of a confined-space explosion, and models that work fine with open-space incidents should not be expected to perform equally well on this scenario. Model 27 (*J. Clutter with Reflection* using *Charles Stewart* injury model) stands out to be the best for this scenario with 80% accuracy, compared to only 47% with Model 13. Model 22 shows no better performance here either, with mere 17.4% accurate prediction.

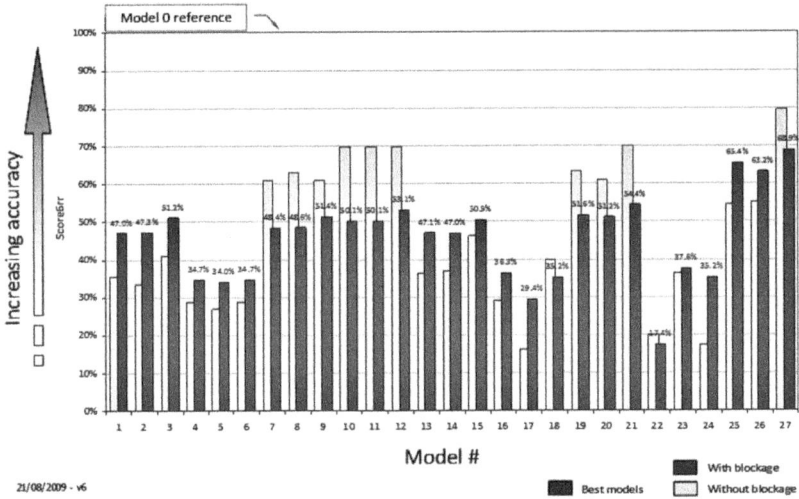

Figure 8.6. Models Cumulative Scoring Performance on Scenario 7.

Figure 8.7 presents Scenario 10. It should be noted that we do not have exact distance data for victims from the suicide bomber, and the results generated by the models are an average of 100 random runs. This is an important case, because it will help us locate a model that can work with minimal input data under a certain confidence of accuracy.

Model 13 stands out as the best model for this scenario as well with 80.6% accuracy compared to only 7.9% for Model 22. This is almost a 75% improvement in prediction performance. There is also an almost 50% accuracy improvement due to the blockage model.

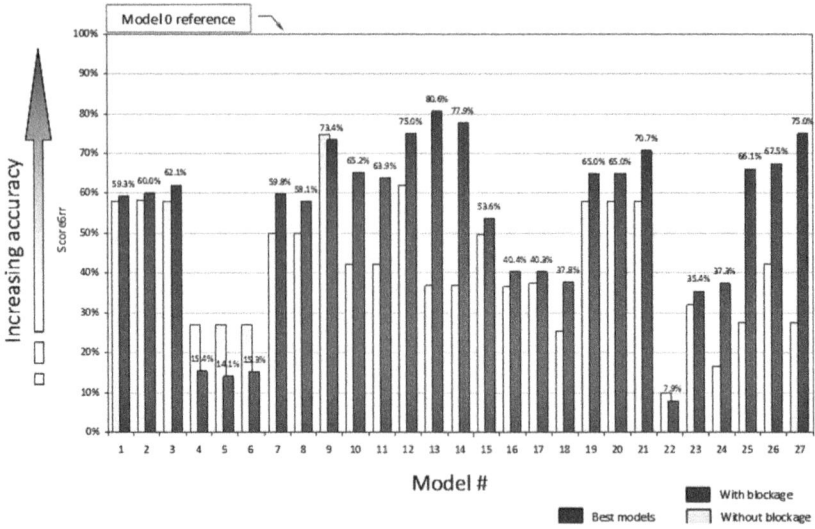

Figure 8.7. Model Cumulative Scoring Performance on Scenario 10.

The best model for open-space scenarios is Model 13 with an accuracy estimate as high as 96%, regardless of the crowd size. This analysis also suggests using Model 27 for confined-space explosion prediction. Model 27 lacks consistency in performance for other scenarios and should only be used with confined-space incidents. Scenario 2 is the best measure to analyze the performance when blockage is present or there is a larger crowd. Scenario 7 is the best predictor for model's performance in confined-space.

8.5.4. Blockage Assessment

This sub-section is focused on determining the impact of using a blockage model in the simulation. Globally, for all scenarios and for all models, the effect of blockage has been assessed with a Mann-Whitney statistical test at 95% confidence. The test confirms a statistically positive effect of the blockage algorithm (p-value$\leq$0.05) for all scoring methods except total count (score5). The median accuracy has increased by nearly 17% while using blockage, as shown in Figure 8.8.

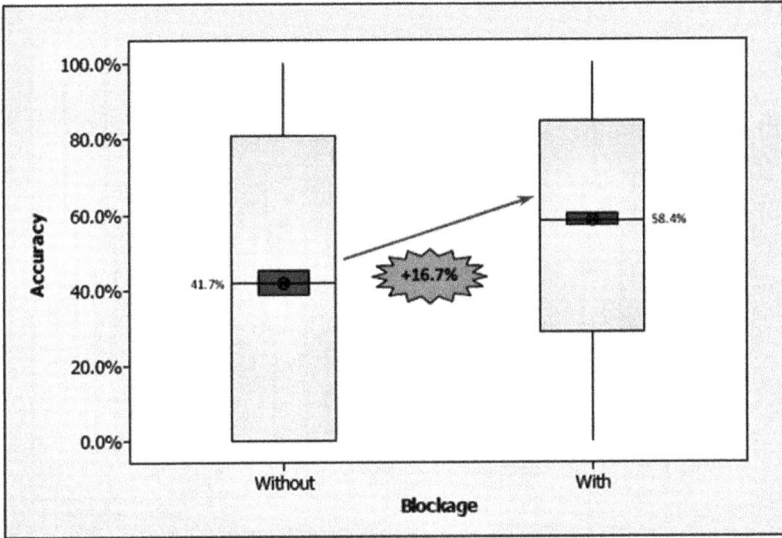

Figure 8.8. Global Blockage Model Assessment on Overall Result.

Different scoring methods yield different performance results. Figure 8.9 shows the performance of blockage model with each scoring method. The algorithm does not affect the total count evaluation (score5), but is of prime interest for the dead count (score2), in comparison to the injury count (score3, score4), and for the weighted accuracy.

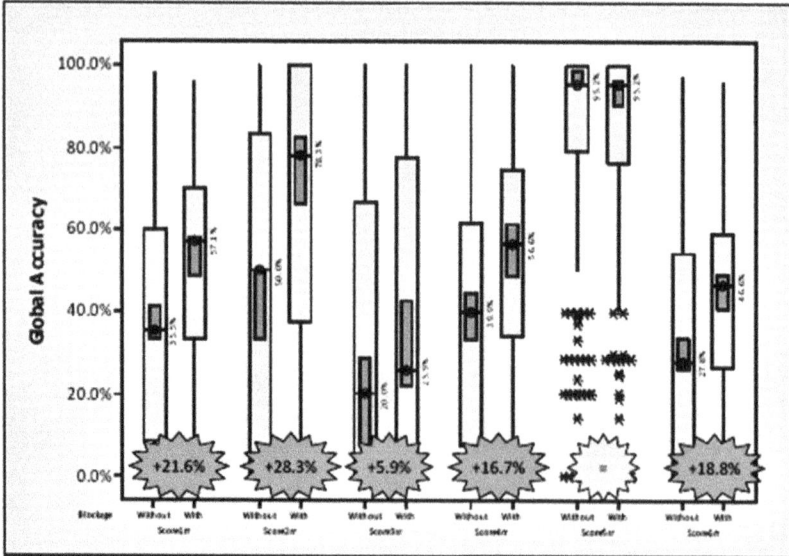

Figure 8.9. Blockage Model Assessment for Each Scoring Method.

Figure 8.10 summarizes the effect of blockage on a model-by-model basis. Unlike previous matrices, the accuracy here is given as a signed value with respect to the actual case reference to see which models over-estimate or under-estimate the counts. It is clear from the figure that blockage generally reduces the scattering and tends to bring the median to the target value of the actual case. Blockage has little or no effect on *Henrych Smith's* models (4, 5, and 6) regardless of the crowd size, and has very little effect on *Harold Brode's* models when used with *ICE* or *Lethality Curve* injury models. For all other models, blockage has a large and significant impact, and is often dramatic when crowd size is more than 100 people.

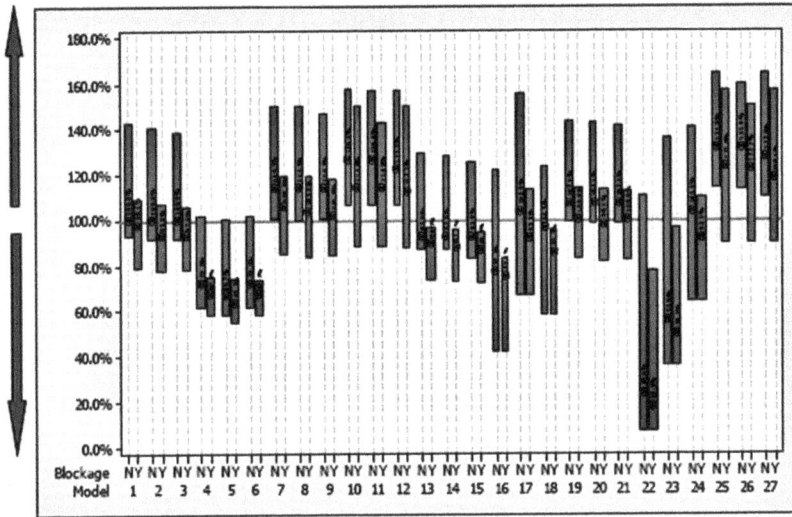

Figure 8.10. Blockage Impact on Each Model.

Figure 8.11 presents the blockage impact on each scenario. Scenario 2 yields the maximum impact of almost 32%. This is not surprising since scenario 2 has the highest number of people in the crowd, and thus the highest number of blockers.

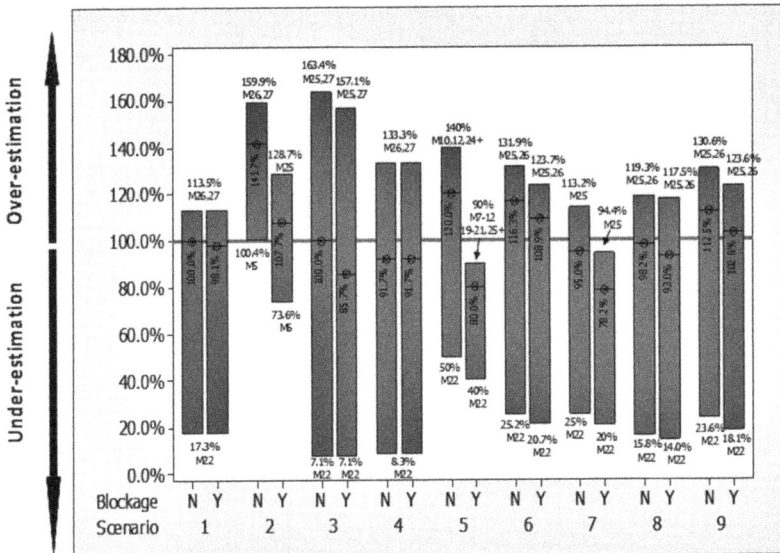

Figure 8.11. Blockage Impact on Scenarios.

8.5.5. Assessing the Impact of Crowd Density

This sub-section discusses the impact of crowd size on global accuracy using the blockage model. Figure 8.12 shows a cumulative impact of crowd size on all models, in all scenarios using the aggregate scoring method. As shown in the figure, model accuracy will linearly increase with the crowd size. The cumulative global accuracy will increase by 14.3% using the blockage model with a crowd size of fewer than 100 people. Due to a lesser number of people, accuracy can dramatically drop depending on the location, human blockage, and the total area available to the crowd. The global accuracy will increase by 41.5% using the blockage model in a crowd size of more than 100 people.

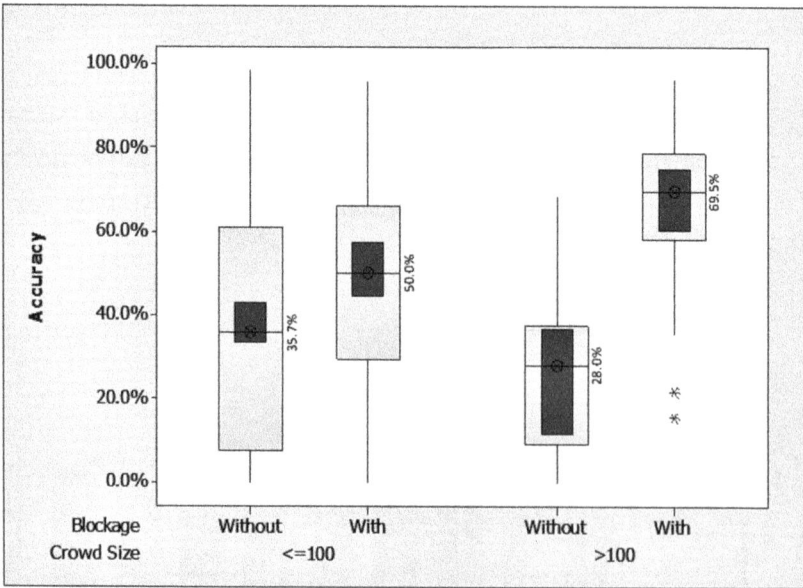

Figure 8.12. Crowd Size Vs. Blockage Accuracy.

Figure 8.13 shows an individual example of Model 13 using a blockage model with different crowd sizes. There is a slight increase of only 1.2% in accuracy with fewer than 100 people. The median range is quite wide here, and a difference of even one person can have a significant impact. The accuracy will increase y 38.3% when there is a crowd size of more than 100 people.

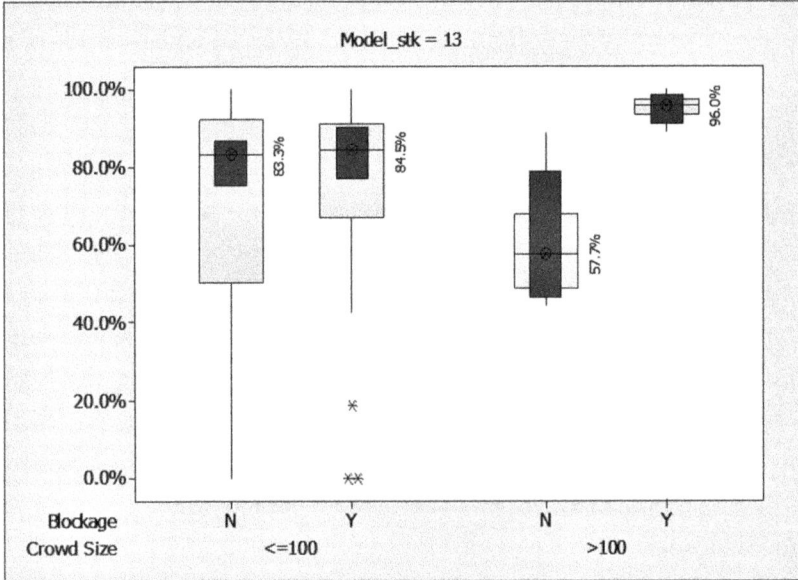

Figure 8.13. Blockage Impact on Scenarios.

No matter what the model or crowd size, there is a significant improvement in accuracy using the blockage model. The best performing models so far are 13, 14, and 15, which gain the most from the blockage model. These also show an enormous increase in accuracy with a larger crowd of more than 100 people.

8.5.6. Sensitivity Analysis

Despite the four-tier authenticity criteria we have used to verify the data collected for the real-life scenarios, we have performed the sensitivity analysis by allowing an error in three important parameters, as described below, for each scenario.

- **TNT Weight:** an explosive weight can be ±2 Kg of TNT

- **Victim to Bomber Distance:** The distance of each victim from the bomber can be ±3 feet

- **Orientation of Victims from the Bomber:** a victim can face towards or away from the bomber, or can be on either side of his/her body

The respective units' range for the above parameters allows us to have a series of new datasets. We have performed our analysis using the best-worst case approach, where the best case means the bomber has the lowest weight of explosive (-2 Kg of the actual weight), victims are farthest away from the bomber (+3 feet of the actual distance), and were oriented parallel to the bomber (facing towards the bomber) and providing the highest possible blockage. In contrast, the worst case means that the bomber has the highest explosive weight (+2 Kg), victims are closer to the bomber (-3 feet), and are oriented perpendicular to the bomber, thus providing little or no blockage.

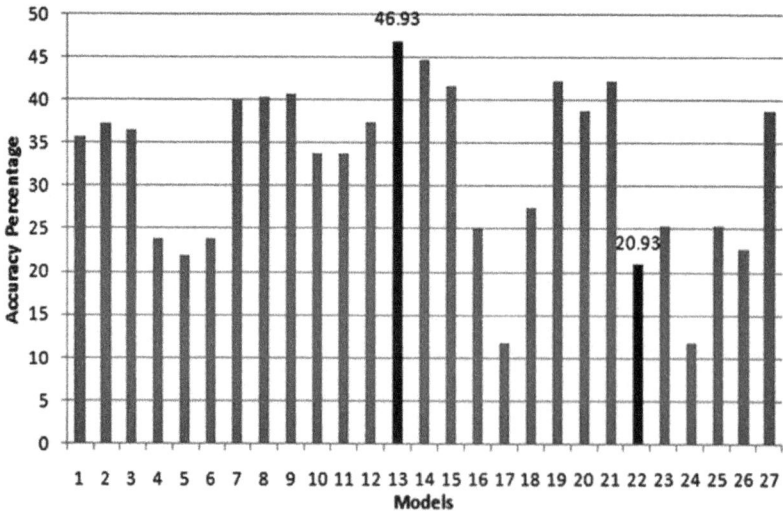

Figure 8.14. Model Performance with Sensitivity Analysis.

Figure 8.14 shows average accuracy for model prediction over actual counts using all best-modeled-worst case situations. Model 13 stands out again with 46.93% of accuracy even when we allowed the aforementioned errors in the data. Model 22 trails behind with 20.93%. This is an important finding that indicates Model 13 should be used when data is not error-free. Overall *Henrych Smith's* model performs better in worst case conditions, and models 17, 24, and 26 perform better in the best case.

8.6. Conclusion

This chapter presented an evaluation of all of the proposed models comparing them to the real-life scenarios using various appraisal functions. Model 13 – the Harold Brode explosive model with the Catherine Lee injury model using blockage – stands out consistently to be the best with an overall cumulative accuracy of 87.6%. Model 27 – the J. Clutter with Reflection using the Charles Stewart injury model with blockage – works best for confined-space incidents (Scenario 7). Model 21 performs best on Scenario 8, but did not show any consistency in performance over the other scenarios. Model 13 is, on average, 70% more accurate than Model 22. Along with Model 22, Models 4, 6, 17, 24, 25, and 26 presented the poorest results over all scenarios. Shortly after Model 13, Models 1 to 3 with Kinney Gilbert's equations are the next best models. Given the simplicity of the equations used by these models, they can be used for fastest response and implementation.

Blockage increases the accuracy of all models by 17% as a whole. The results are visible whatever the criteria, except for total count (that remains unaffected). Result scattering is also significantly reduced by using the blockage model. The accuracy improvement is also leveraged by the crowd size. When blockage is effective, the effect is 4 times higher with crowds greater than 100 people compared to the smaller crowds.

Model robustness has also been assessed by limited changes in the input parameters as described in the Section 8.4.6. All models revealed high sensitivity to these conditions. Nonetheless, Model 13 turned out to be best tuned, after sensitivity analysis, with almost 47%.

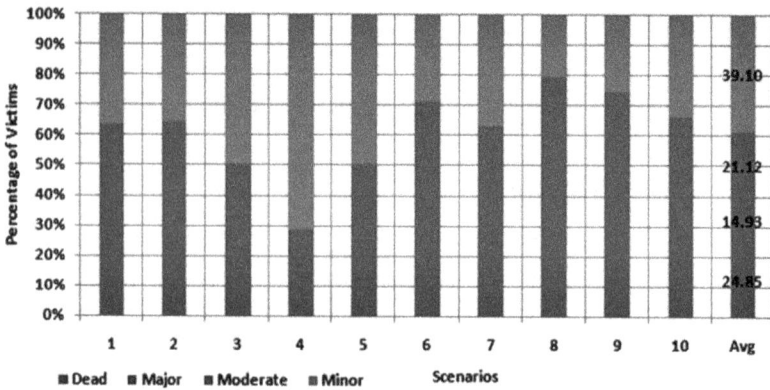

Figure 8.15: Distribution of Injuries by Model 13.

Figure 8.15 presents the percentage distribution of injuries and lethal counts over all 10 scenarios for Model 13. Comparing it with Figure 8.1, Model 13 shows similar results for dead and moderately injured people. The results are 4% off for major injured (remember the special case of Scenario 7), and 15% off for minor injured. There can be many reasons for the poor performance on minor injuries. First of all, the current simulation does not consider tertiary injuries – injuries caused by building collapse, toxic and dust inhalation, previous medical conditions, burns and thermal radiations. Second, most of the minor injured victims with small cuts, bruises and burns leave the area as soon as they can, and are not usually counted in the data available through government agencies and hospital records. We will be incorporating tertiary and miscellaneous blast injuries in future work, and we are hopeful that it will reduce the gap in accuracy prediction for minor injuries.

9. Conclusion and Future Work

The work presented a simulation platform called BlastSim to model the effects of a suicide bombing for a given crowd with various explosive, crowd, environment and blockage characteristics. Twenty seven different model combinations have been tested and evaluated against a real-life database of suicide bombing incidents. The Harold Brode explosive model with Catherine Lee injury model using the blockage consistently stands out to be the best model to predict blast injuries on humans with an overall accuracy of 87.6%. This model combination can increase the prediction accuracy by 71% compare to existing tools based on Bowen's lethality curves for injury prediction. However, it should only be used for open-space scenarios. The J. Clutter explosive model with Charles Stewart injury model using the blockage emerges as a best candidate for confined-space scenarios with an accuracy of 80%.

The blockage model can increase the overall accuracy of all models by 17%. It can be as high as 28% for appraisal functions with only dead counts. The blockage model shifts the victims (within the boundaries of the total count) among various injury and lethality categories for an accurate prediction. The blockage model yields four times better results with a crowd size of more than 100 people. The simulation results with the best models are only 4% off for the major injured counts, but 15% off for minor injured. Addition of tertiary injuries, whole-body-translation, structural collapse, and knowledge of existing medical conditions can surely improve the results. The results can also help to plan for post-disaster management, for example, how many ambulances and doctors are required for a crowd of given size in case of a suicide bombing attack.

There is an acute shortage of accurate data for many other variables and conditions that are pertinent to such attacks (e.g. was bomber running or standing? Carrying methods for the explosive? Victims' existing medical conditions, age, weight and height? etc.). More data on suicide bombing from other parts of the world can surely help to refine the results and make this simulation an ultimate tool for emergency managers throughout the world.

We would like to include tertiary injuries, whole-body-translation due to the blast impact, structural collapse, debris, plug-n-play fragmentation models, and objects like cars and trees in the future versions. Simulated Injury Scores (SIS) will be added in the future as well. SIS will follow the criteria used by other injury severity scores like Abbreviated Injury Scale (AIS), Injury Severity Score (ISS), Trauma Score, Glasgow Coma Score, and an extension of AIS called Anatomic Profile (AP). These scaling and scores will help in triage for victims based on magnitude of their injuries and the probability of their survivals. These scores can be further used for statistical studies and to co-relate with blast characteristics to establish an approximate measure of damage [Robertson 2007]. Furthermore, we are also working on an advance interrogation methods for scenario characteristics to improve the prediction accuracy. For example, a typical suicide bombing incident contains number of people in an open-space and quite a few in confined-space (such as cars, buildings) or nearby a reflection surface (such as walls and other objects). Our advance algorithm is intelligent enough to treat a crowd based on their surroundings, so ones who are in open-space will be treated by an open-space model, while those who are nearby a reflection surface will be analyzed by a reflection model. Our initial results suggests a significant performance increase.

The simulation and findings are limited in that they only incorporate the primary and secondary injuries. Future plans are to add tertiary effects (e.g., injuries by fire, debris, etc.) to better approximate the real-world environment and provide more valid comparisons with the data of suicide bombing attack aftermath. It is also hard to classify injuries based on their mechanism, for almost all of the injuries result from a combination of multiple factors, like blast overpressure, fragmentation, projectiles and shrapnel, whole body translation, carbon monoxide poisoning, or chronic illness aggravated by explosion, to name a few. Furthermore, there is very limited data available for indoor victims of an explosion. There is no scientifically proven way to scale or extrapolate outdoor impact to indoor inmates for explosions like suicide bombing [Davies 1993]. Therefore, the results generated by this simulation will be of less importance for explosions in confined space. This work provides an interesting direction for future research to investigate the catastrophic event of a suicide bombing attack in hopes of making the world a safer place.

References

Abbasi, S. A., and Khan, F. I., "DOMIFFECT (DOMIno eFFECT): user-friendly software for domino effect analysis", Elsevier Journal of Environmental Modeling and Software, Volume 13, pp: 163-177, 1998

Abdel-Gayed, R. G., Bradley, D., and Lawes, M., "Turbulent burning velocities: a general correlation in terms of straining rates", Proceedings of the Royal Society of London, A414:389-413, 1987

Aizik, F., Ben-Dor, G., Elperin, T., and Igra, O., "Spherical Shock Waves – General Attenuation Law for Spherical Shock Wave Propagation in Pure Gases", Handbook of Shock Waves, Vol. 2, 2001

Al-Muqrin, A., "A Practical Course for Guerrila War", Translated by Norman Cigar with the title "Al-Qaida's Doctrine For Insurgency", Potomac Books Inc., Washington D.C, 2008

Arienti, M., Huld, T., and Wilkening, H., "An adaptive 3-D CFD solver for simulating large scale chemical explosions", Proceedings of the 4th ECCOMAS Computational Fluid Dynamics conference, 7-11 September, Athens, Greece, 1998

Arntzen, B. J., "Combustion Modeling in FLACS 93", HSE Offshore Technology Report, OTN 95 220, 1995

Arntzen, B. J., "Modeling of turbulence and combustion for simulation of gas explosions in complex geometries", Dr. Ing. Thesis, Norges Tekniske-Naturvitenskapelige Universitet, Trondheim, Norway Baker, 1998

Azam, J., "Suicide-bombing as inter- generational investment", Public Choice. Springer. 122, 177-198, 2005

Baker, Q. A., Doolittle, C. M., Fitzgerald, G. A., and Tang, M. J., "Recent developments in the Baker-Strehlow VCE Analysis Methodology", Process Safety Progress 17(4):297-301, 1998

Baker, Q. A., Tang, M. J., Scheier, E. A., and Silva, G. J., "Vapor Cloud Explosion Analysis", AIChE Loss Prevention Symposium, Atlanta, Georgia, U.S.A, 1994

Baker, W. E., Cox, P. A., Westine, P. S., Kulesz, J. J., and Strehlow, R. A., "Explosion Hazards and Evaluation", Elsevier, 1983

Baker, W.E., "Explosions in Air", University of Texas Press, Austin, TX, 1973

Benzinger, T., "Physiological effects of blast in air and water", In reference 43, 1225-1259, 1950

Berg, A. C., "The Multi-Energy Method - A Framework for Vapor Cloud Explosion Blast Prediction", Journal of Hazardous Materials, 12:1-10, 1985

Beshara, F. B. A., "Modeling of blast loading on aboveground structures – I. General Phenomenology and external blast", Comp. and Structures. Vol. 51, No. 5, Pergamon Press Inc. Tarrytown, NY, pp. 597-606, June 3, 1994

Birkby, P., Cant, R. S., and Savill, A. M., "Initial HSE Baffled Channel Test Case Results with Refined Combustion and Turbulence Modeling", 1st Milestone Report on the HSE Research Contract Research at Cambridge University under Agreement No. HSE/8685/3278, 1997

Bjerketvedt, D., Bakke, J. R., and Wingerden, K. V., "Gas Explosion Handbook", Journal Hazardous Materials 52:1-150, 1997

Bogosian, D., Ferritto, J., and Shi, Y., "Measuring Uncertainty and Conservatism in Simplified Blast Models", 30th Explosive Safety Seminar, Atlanta, GA, August 2002

Born, C. T., "Blast Trauma: The Fourth Weapon of Mass Destruction", Scandinavian Journal of Surgery, Vol 94, pp. 279-285, 2005

Bowen, G., Fletcher, E. R., and Richmond, D. R., "Estimate of Man's Tolerance to the Direct Effects of Air Blast", Defense Atomic Support Agency Report, Headquarters, Washington D.C, October, 1968

Bray, K. , and Moss, J., "A Unified Statistical Model of the Turbulent Premixed Flame", Acta Astronautica 4:291-320, 1977

Bray, K., "Studies of the turbulent burning velocity", Proceedings of the Royal Society of London A431:315-325, 1990

Bray, K., Champion, M., and Libby, P., "The Interaction Between Turbulence and Chemistry in Premixed Turbulent Flames Turbulent Reactive Flows", Lecture Notes in Engineering No. 40, Springer Verlag, pp. 541-563, 1989

Bray, K., Libby, P., and Moss, J., "Unified Modeling Approach for Premixed Turbulent Combustion", Part 1: General Formulation Combustion and Flame, 61:87-102, 1985

Brode, Harold, "Numerical Solutions of Spherical Blast Waves," Journal of Applied Physics, Vol. 26, 766(1955); "A Calculation of the Blast Wave from a Spherical Charge of TNT.", Santa Monica: The RAND Corporation, 1957

Briggs, S., "Advanced Disaster Medical Response – Manual for Providers", Harvard Medical International Trauma and Disaster Institute, Boston, MA, 2003

Cates, A. T., and Samuels, B., "A Simple Assessment Methodology for Vented Explosions", Journal of Loss Prevention in the Process Industries 4:287-296, 1991

Catlin, C. A., and Lindstedt, R. P., "Premixed Turbulent Burning Velocities Derived from Mixing Controlled Reaction Models with Cold Front Quenching", Combustion and Flame, 85:427-439, 1991

Catlin, C. A., Fairweather, M., and Ibrahim, S. S., "Predictions of Turbulent, Premixed Flame Propagation in Explosion Tubes", Combustion and Flame, 102:115-128, 1995

Chippett, S., "Modeling of Vented Deflagrations", Combustion and Flame 55:127-140, 1984

Ciraulo, David. L., and Frykberg, E. R., "The Surgeon and Acts of Civilian Terrorism" Blast Injuries", Journal of American College of Surgeons, ISSN 1072-7515/06, 2006

Clutter, J. K., Mathis, J. T., and Stahl, M. W., "Modeling Environmental effects in the Simulation of Explosion Events", International Journal of Impact Engineering, March 2006

Cooper, P. W., "Explosive Engineering", Wiley-VCH, 1996

Crabtree, J., "Terrorist Homicide Bombings: A Primer for Preparation", Journal of Burn Care Research, American Burn Association, Vol. 27, Issue 5, October 2006

121

David, T. E., "An Introduction to Asymmetric War (Terrorism) and the Epidemiology of Blast Trauma", Presentation at Emory University, 2008

Davies, P. A., "A guide to the Evaluation of Condensed Phase Explosions", Journal of Hazardous Materials, Vol. 33, pp. 1-33, 1993

DePalma, R. G., Burris, D. G., and Champion, H. R., "Blast Injuries", The New England Journal of Medicine 352:13, March 31, 2005

Dire, D. J., "Conventional Terrorist Bombings", Chapter 32 of Section 5, "Conflict Related Disasters", in "Disaster Medicine", Hogan, David. E. (Editor), Lippincott Williams & Wilkins; Second Edition, New York, NY, March 1, 2007

Ettouney, M., "Is Seismic Design Adequate for Blast?", Society of American Military Engineers National Symposium on Comprehensive Force Protection, Charleston, S.C., November 2001

Fairweather, M., and Vasey, M. W., "A Mathematical Model for the Prediction of Overpressures Generated in Totally Confined and Vented Explosions", 19th Symposium (International) on Combustion, The Combustion Institute, Pittsburgh, Pennsylvania, U.S.A., pp. 645-653, 1982

Fairweather, M., Hargrave, G. K., Ibrahim, S. S., and Walker, D. G., "Studies of Premixed Flame Propagation in Explosion Tubes", Combustion and Flame 116(4):504-518, 1999

Fairweather, M., Ibrahim, S. S., Jaggers, H. and Walker, D.G., " Turbulent Premixed Flame Propagation in a Cylindrical Vessel", 26th Symposium (International) on Combustion, The Combustion Institute, Pittsburgh, Pennsylvania, U.S.A., pp. 365-371, 1996

FEMA (Federal Emergency Management Association), "Designer's Notebook – Blast Consideration", FEMA Press, 2006

FEMA (Federal Emergency Management Association), "Explosive Blast Manual", Section 4.1. FEMA Press, 2004

Ferris, J., "Forensics Pathology of Victims of an Explosion", Book chapter in "Forensic Investigation of Explosions", by Alexander Beveridge (editor).,Taylor and Francis, 1998

Fertal, M., and Leone, K., "Applications of Blast/FX – An Explosive Effects Analysis Software Tool", IEEE 34th Annual 2000 International Carnahan Conference on Security Technology, Ottawa, ON, Canada, October 23 - 25, 2000

Foltin, G. L., "Pediatric Terrorism and Disaster Preparedness – a Resource for Pediatricians", American Academy of Pediatrics, 2006

Freeman, D. J., " Visualization of explosions in a baffled plate vented enclosure", HSL Report IR/L/GE/94/08, 1994

Ganor, B., "Suicide Attacks in Israel", In: Ganor, B., (ed.), "Countering Suicide Terrorism", Herliya, Israel, Interdisciplinary Center Publishing House, pp. 134, 2001

Ganor, B., "The Rationality of the Islamic Radical Suicide Attack Phenomenon", Countering Suicide Terrorism, Institute of Counter Terrorism, 2000

Garth, R. J. N., "Blast Injury of the Auditory System: A Review of the Mechanisms and Pathology", The Journal of LO, November, Vol 108, pp. 925-929, 1994

Gilbert, K., and Kenneth, G., "Explosive Shocks in Air", 2nd Sub edition. Springer, 1985

Glasstone, S., and Dolan, P. J., "The Effects of Nuclear Weapons", 3rd Edition, Washington D.C, US Department of Defense, 1977

Godunov, S. K., "A Finite Difference Method for the Computation of Discontinuous Solutions of the Equations of Fluid Dynamics", Mat. Sb. 47:271-290, 1959

Greer, A. D., "Numerical Modeling for the Prediction of Primary Blast Injury to the Lung", Master's Thesis, University of Waterloo, Ontario, Canada, 2006

Greer, A., Cronin, C., Salisbury, C., and Williams, K., "Finite Element Modeling for the Prediction of Blast Trauma", Gilchrist, Michael. D., (ed.), "IUTAM Proceedings on Impact Biomechanics: from Fundamental Insights to Applications", pp. 263-271, 2005

Gupta, D. K., and Mundra, K., "Suicide Bombing as a Strategic Weapon: An Empirical Investigation of Hamas and Islamic Jihad. Terrorism and Political Violence", 17, 573-598, 2005

Harrison, M., "Bombers and Bystanders in Suicide Attacks in Isreal 2000 to 2003", Studies in Conflict and Terrorism. 29, 187-206, 2006

Harrison, M., "The Immediate Effects of Suicide Attacks", University of Warwick, 2004

Hjertager, B. H.' "Numerical Simulation of Flame and Pressure Development in Gas Explosions", SM study no. 16, University of Waterloo Press, Ontario, Canada, pp. 407-426, 1982

Hulek, T., and Lindstedt, R. P., "Computations of Steady-State and Transient Premixed Turbulent Flames Using pdf Methods", Combustion and Flame, 104:481-506, 1996

ICE, "Explosions in the Process Industries", A report of the Major Hazards Assessment Panel Overpressure Working Party, 2nd Edition, Institution of Chemical Engineers (ICE), 1994

Irwin, R. J., Lerner, M. R., Bealer, J. F., Mantor, P. C., Brackett, D. J., and Tuggle, D. W., "Shock after blast wave injury is caused by a vagally mediated reflex", Journal of Trauma, Volume 47, p. 105-110, 1999

Joachim, C. E., McMahon, G. W., Lunderman, C. V., and Garner, S. B., "Air blast Effects Research: Small-Scale Experiments and Calculations", Technical Report SL-99-5, Army Material Command, Special Projects Support Activity, Fort Belvoir, Virginia, August 1999

Johnson, D. L., "Overpressure Studies with Animals and Man: Non-auditory Damage Risk Assessment for Simulated 155mm Self-Propelled Howitzer Blast", Final Report for U.S. Army Medical Research and Material Command, For Derrick, Maryland, 2000

Jones, W. P., "Models for turbulent flows with variable density and combustion", in: "Prediction Methods for Turbulent Flows", (Ed.: Kollmann W.), Hemisphere, Washington D.C., U.S.A., pp. 423-458, 1980

Krauthammer, T., "Modern Protective Structures (Civil and Environmental Engineering)", CRC Press, February 2008

Kress, M., "The Effect of Crowd Density on the Expected Number of Casualties in a Suicide Attack", Wiley Periodicals, 2004

Lea, C. J., "A Review of the State-of-the-Art in Gas Explosion Modeling", Technical Report Royal Health and Safety Laboratory, Buxton, Scotland, 2004

Lee, C. Y., "Survey of Blast Trauma from Evolving Tactics of Terrorism", Presentation at New York Medical College, October 17 2005

Lee, C. Y., "Survey of Terrorist Bombing Tactics and How they influence patterns of Injury", Emory University, Department of Emergency Medicine, 2008.

Leer, B. V., "Flux Vector Splitting for the Euler Equations", Lecture Notes in Physics, Springer-Verlag, 170:507-51, 1982

Leer, B. V., "Towards the Ultimate Conservative Difference Scheme", Section II. Monotonicity and Conservation Combined in a Second-Order Scheme, Journal of Computational Physics 14:361-370, 1974

Lenz, R., "Explosive and Bomb Disposal Guide", Charles C. Thomas Publishers, Springfield, IL, 1976

Lester, D., Yang, B., and Lindsay, M., "Suicide Bombers: Are Psychological Profiles Possible?", Studies in Conflict and Terrorism. 27, 283-295, 2004

Limor, A., and Shapira, S. C., "Epidemiology of Terrorism Injuries", Chapter 10 in Shapira, S. C. (ed.), "Essentials of Terror Medicine" Springer Verlag, 2009

Lindstedt, R. P., and Váos, E. M., "Second Moment Modeling of Premixed Turbulent Flames Stabilized in Impinging Jet Geometries", 27th Symposium (International) on Combustion, The Combustion Institute, Pittsburgh, Pennsylvania, U.S.A., pp. 957-962, 1998

Lindstedt, R. P., Hulek, T., and Váos, E. M., "Further Development of Numerical Sub-models and Theoretical Support", EMERGE Project Report, 1997

Linsky, R., and Miller, A., "Types of Explosions and Explosive Injuries Defined", Chapter # 20, of Section 5, "Explosive and Traumatic Terrorism", in "Medical Response to Terrorism – Preparedness and Clinical Practice", Keyes, Daniel. C. (Editor), Lippincott Williams and Wilkins, New York, NY, 2006

Lovelace, foundation for Medical Education and Research, "Biological Blast Effects", Albuquerque, New Mexico, June 1959

Mahoney, P. F., Ryan, J. M., and Brooks, A. J., "Ballistic Trauma – A Practical Guide", second edition, Springer Verlag, 2009

Marti, M., and Parron, M., "Blast Injuries from Madrid Terrorist Bombing Attacks on March 11, 2004", Emergency Radiology, 13:113-122, 2006

Martins, C., Buchanan, J., and Amanatides, J., "Visually Believable Explosions in Real Time", IEEE 2001.

Mayo, A., and Kluger, Y., "Terrorist Bombing", World Journal of Emergency Surgery, Vol 1, Issue 33., November 2006

McKean, J. W., and Ryan, T. A. Jr., "An Algorithm for Obtaining Confidence Intervals and Point Estimates Based on Ranks in the Two Sample Location Problem," Transactions on Mathematical Software, pp.183-185, 1977

Mellor, S.G., and Cooper, G. J., "Analysis of 828 servicemen killed or injured by explosion in Northern Ireland 1970-1984", The hostile Action Casualty System. Br Journal of Surgery Vol. 76, pp. 1006-1010, 1989

Mercx, W. P. M., "Modeling and experimental research into gas explosions: overall final report on the MERGE project", Commission of the European Communities Report, Contract STEP-CT-011 (SSMA), 1993

Mercx, W. P. M., and Berg, A. C., "The Explosion Blast Prediction Model in the Revised CPR 14E", (Yellow Book), Process Safety Progress 16(3):152-159, 1997

Mohanty, B., "Physics of Explosion Hazards", Book chapter in "Forensic Investigation of Explosions", by Alexander Beveridge (editor).,Taylor and Francis, 1998

Moore, B., "Blast Injuries – A Pre-hospital Perspective", Journal of Emergency Primary Health Care (JEPHC), Vol. 4, Issue 1, 2006

NATO (North Atlantic Treaty Organization), "RTO Technical Report - TR-HFM-090", Final Report of HFM-090 Task Group 25, Test Methodology for Protection of Vehicle Occupants against Anti-Vehicular Landmine Effects, 2007

NATO, "Reconsideration of the effects of impulse noise", RTO Technical report TR-017 AC/323, 2003

Newmark, N. M., "An Engineering Approach to Blast Resistant Design", Proceedings of ASCE, 1979

Noon, R. K., "Forensic Engineering Investigation", CRC Press, New York, NY 2000

Oladitoye, O., "A Representative Survey of Blast Loading Models and Damage Assessment Methods for Buildings Subject To Explosive Blasts", CEWES MSRC/PET TR/98-36, 1998

Palmer, G., "Physics for Game Developers, Chapter 13th, Academic Press, New York, 2005

Pape, R. A., "Dying to Win: The Strategic Logic of Suicide Terrorism", Random House, 2005

Patankar, S. V., and Spalding, D. B., "A Calculation Procedure for Heat, Mass and Momentum Transfer in Three-dimensional Parabolic Flows", International Journal of Heat and Mass Transfer 15:1787-1806, 1972

Popat, N. R., Catlin, C. A., Arntzen, B. J., Lindstedt, R. P., Hjertager, B. H., Solberg, T., Sæter, O., and Berg, A. C., "Investigations to Improve and Assess the Accuracy of Computational Fluid Dynamic Based Explosion Models", Journal of Hazardous Materials 45:1-25, 1996

Pritchard, D. K., "A Review of Methods for Predicting Blast Damage from Vapor Cloud Explosions", Journal of Loss Prevention, Volume 2, October 1989

Pritchard, D. K., Freeman, D. J., and Guilbert, P. W., "Prediction of Explosion Pressures in Confined Spaces", Journal of Loss Prevention in the Process Industries 9:205-215, 1996

Pritchard, D. K., Lewis, M. J., Hedley, D., and Lea, C. J., "Predicting the effect of obstacles on explosion development", HSL Report No. EC/99/41 - CM/99/11, 1999

Puttock, J. S., "Fuel Gas Explosion Guidelines - the Congestion Assessment Method", 2nd European Conference on Major Hazards On- and Off-shore, Manchester, UK, 24-26 September 1995

Puttock, J. S., "Improvements in Guidelines for Prediction of Vapor-cloud Explosions", International Conference and Workshop on Modeling the Consequences of Accidental Releases of Hazardous Materials, San Francisco, Sept-Oct, 1999

Puttock, J. S., Cresswell, T. M., Marks, P. R., Samuels, B., and Prothero, A., "Explosion Assessment in Confined Vented Geometries", SOLVEX Large-Scale Explosion Tests and SCOPE Model Development HSE Offshore Technology Report, OTO 96 004, 1996

Puttock, J. S., Yardley, M. R., and Cresswell, T. M., "Prediction of Vapor Cloud Explosions Using the SCOPE Model", Journal of Loss Prevention in the Process Industries 13:419-430, 2000

Rawlins, J. S. P, "Physical and Patho-physiological effects of Blast", Journal of Royal Naval Scientific Service, Vol. 29, 1977

Resse, R. L., "University Physics", Chapter 12, "Waves", Brooks/Cole Publishing Company, 2000

Rice, D., & Heck, J. "Terrorist bombings: Ballistics, patterns of blast injury and tactical emergency care". The Tactical Edge Journal, Summer, 53-55, 2000

Robertson, L., "Injury Epidemiology: Research and Control Strategies", Oxford University Press, USA; 3 edition, July 3, 2007

Roe, P. L., "Approximate Riemann Solvers, Parameter Vectors, and Difference Schemes", Journal of Computational Physics 43:357-372, 1981

Rogers, G. L., "Dynamics of Framed Structures", John Wiley, New York, 1959

Selby, C. A., and Burgan, B. A., "Blast and Fire Engineering for Topside Structures - Phase 2 (Final Summary Report)", SCI Publication No. 253, The Steel Construction Institute, Ascot, U.K, 1998

Serge, N., and Comton, J., "Integration Study of Prospective Hazards Models for the Enhancement of a Virtual Range Simulation Model", Proceedings of the 2005 Winter Simulation Conference, 2005

Sharpnack, D. D., Johnson, A. J., and Phillips, Y. Y., "The Pathology of blast Injury", in Bellamy, R.F, and Zajtcjuk, J. Y., eds., "Conventional Warfare: Ballistic, blast, and burn injuries", Washington D.C, Office of the Surgeon General at TMM Publications, 1991

Simmonds, K. E., Matic, P., Chase, M., and Leung, A., "GelMan.: A Physical Model for Measuring the Response to Blast", 2001

Singer, P., Cohen, J. D., and Stein, M., "Conventional Terrorism and Critical Care", Critical Care Medicine, Vol. 33, Issue 1, Supplement, 2005

Stein, M, "Urban Bombing: A Trauma Surgeon's Perspective", Scandinavian Journal of Surgery, Vol 94, pp. 286-292, 2005

Stein, M., and Hirsberg, A., "Medical Consequences of Terrorism – The Conventional Weapon Threat", Trauma Center in the new Millenium, Vol. 79, Issue 6, December 1999

Stewart, C., "Blast Injuries: Preparing for the Inevitable", Emergency Medicine Practice, An Evidence-Based Approach to Emergency Medicine, Vol. 8, Issue. 4, April 2006

Stiglitz, J. E., and Bilmes, L. J., "The Three Trillion Dollar War – The True Cost of the Iraq Conflict", W. W. Norton & Company, New York, NY 2008

Strehlow, R. A., and Baker, W. E., "The Characterization and Evaluation of Accidental Explosions", Prog. Energy, Combustion, Science, Vol 2, pp. 27-60, Pentagon Press, UK, 1976

Strehlow, R. A., Luckritz, R. T., Adamczyk, A. A., and Shimpi, S. A., "The Blast Wave Generated by Spherical Flames", Combustion and Flame 35:297-310, 1979

Tang, Q. A., Scheier, M. J., and Silva, G. J., "Vapor Cloud Explosion Analysis", AIChE Loss Prevention Symposium, Atlanta, Georgia, 1994

Thurman, J. T., "Practical Bomb Scene Investigation", Taylor and Francis, New York, NY, 2006

Thyer, A. M., "Updates to VCE Modeling for Flammable Risk", at: Part 1 HSL Report No. RAS/97/04 - FS/97/01, 1997

Usmani, Z., and Kirk, D., "How Much a Programmer Worth? – Introducing Personal Worth Indicator", The 2009 International Conference on Software Engineering Research and Practice (SERP' 09), Las Vegas, NV, 2009

Usmani, Z., and Kirk, D., "Suicide Bombing – National Survey of Pakistan", Working paper 2009.

Walter, P. L., "Air-Blast and the Science of Dynamic Pressure Measurements", Sound and Vibration, December 2004

Watterson, J. K., Connell, I. J., Savill A. M., and Dawes, W. N., "A Solution-Adaptive Mesh Procedure for Predicting confined Explosions", International Journal for Numerical Methods in Fluids 26:235-247, 1998

Watterson, J. K., Savill, A. M, Dawes, W. N., and Bray, K. N. C., "Predicting Confined Explosions with an Unstructured Adaptive Mesh Code", Joint Meeting of the Portuguese, British and Spanish Sections of the Combustion Institute, 1996

White, C. S., "Biological Blast Effects", USAEC Report TID-5564. Lovelace Foundation for Medical Education and Research, 1959

Wiekema, B. J., "Vapor Cloud Explosion Model", Journal of Hazardous Materials 3:221-232, 1980

Wilkening, H., and Huld, T., "An adaptive 3-D CFD solver for explosion modeling on large scales", 17th International Colloquium on the Dynamics of Explosions and Reactive Systems, Heidelberg, Germany, July 25-30, 1999

Wingerden, K. V., "Developments in Gas Explosion Safety in the 1990's", in Norway FABIG Newsletter, Article R397, Issue no. 28 (April 2001), pp. 17-20, 2001

Zorpette, G., "Countering IEDs", IEEE Spectrum, pp. 27-35, September 2008

About the Authors

Zeeshan-ul-hassan Usmani: Dr. Usmani is a Fulbright Scholar. He holds a PhD and MS in Computer Science from the Florida Institute of Technology. As part of his Master's thesis, he has developed a simulation of supermarkets to observe and quantify the effects of herd behavior on impulse shopping by customers. His PhD work focuses on simulation and modeling of blast waves in open and confined spaces. His work has been mentioned in Wall Street Journal, AOL News, Wired Magazine, NPR, MIT's Technology Review, Florida Today, and The Economist. He has authored dozens of research papers, articles, and three books. His research strengths include real-world simulation, programming human emergent behaviors, and modeling of catastrophic events. He has worked in Citi Bank New York, Discover Financials, Illinois, Fulbright Academy of Science and Technology in Maine, and at the department of computer science at GIK Institute, Topi, Pakistan. Currently, he is working as a Chief of Research at Interactive Group in Islamabad, where he lives with his wife and three kids.

Daniel Kirk: Dr. Daniel R. Kirk is an associate professor in the Mechanical and Aerospace Engineering Department at the Florida Institute of Technology. Prior to joining Florida Tech in 2004, he completed his doctorate of philosophy (Ph.D.) and a post-doctoral fellowship at the Massachusetts Institute of Technology (MIT) in the Department of Aeronautics and Astronautics under a National Science Foundation Fellowship. Prior to his graduate work at MIT, he was the Valedictorian of the class of 1997 at the Rensselaer Polytechnic Institute where he majored in mechanical engineering with minors in astronomy and philosophy. Dr. Kirk's research interests focus on propulsion, combustion, and blast-structure interactions. He has produced over 50 conference and journal publications, served as a visiting scholar at NASA Marshall Space Flight Center and NASA Kennedy Space Center and has managed research projects with NASA, the U.S. Air Force, and the Office of Naval Research. Dr. Kirk has won numerous teaching awards, culminating in 2008 with the prestigious Society of Automotive Engineers (SAE) Ralph A. Teetor award for integration of research and teaching. In 2009 he was selected as a Boeing Welliver Faculty Fellow. Dr. Kirk is a member of the America Institute of Aeronautics and Astronautics (AIAA), SAE, Sigma Xi, The Scientific Research Society, and Tau Beta Pi, the National Engineering Honor Society. Dr. Kirk enjoys studying the Polish and Russian languages, playing baseball, tennis, surfing, snowboarding, chess, and he is currently training to compete in his 7th marathon.

Lightning Source UK Ltd.
Milton Keynes UK
UKHW012104221222
414360UK00004B/39